National Styles in Science, Diplomacy, and Science Diplomacy

Diplomacy and Foreign Policy

Editor-in-Chief

Corneliu Bjola (*University of Oxford*)

Associate Editors

Wilfried Bolewski (*American Graduate School* in *Paris*)
Caitlin Byrne (*Director of the Griffith Asia Institute, Australia*)
Cathryn A. Clüver (*Harvard University*)
Jorge Heine (*Ambassador of Chile to the People's Republic of China*)
Marcus Holmes (*College of William & Mary*)
Stuart Murray (*Bond University*)
Qingmin Zhang (*Peking University*)

Volumes published in this Brill Research Perspective are listed at *brill.com/rpdf*

National Styles in Science, Diplomacy, and Science Diplomacy

By

Olga Krasnyak

BRILL

LEIDEN | BOSTON

Originally published as Volume 3.1 (2018), in *Diplomacy and Foreign Policy*, DOI:10.1163/24056006-12340009.

Library of Congress Control Number: 2018963439

Typeface for the Latin, Greek, and Cyrillic scripts: "Brill". See and download: brill.com/brill-typeface.

ISBN 978-90-04-39443-8 (paperback)
ISBN 978-90-04-39444-5 (e-book)

Copyright 2019 by Olga Krasnyak. Published by Koninklijke Brill NV, Leiden, The Netherlands.
Koninklijke Brill NV incorporates the imprints Brill, Brill Hes & De Graaf, Brill Nijhoff, Brill Rodopi, Brill Sense, Hotei Publishing, mentis Verlag, Verlag Ferdinand Schöningh and Wilhelm Fink Verlag.
Koninklijke Brill NV reserves the right to protect the publication against unauthorized use and to authorize dissemination by means of offprints, legitimate photocopies, microform editions, reprints, translations, and secondary information sources, such as abstracting and indexing services including databases. Requests for commercial re-use, use of parts of the publication, and/or translations must be addressed to Koninklijke Brill NV.

This book is printed on acid-free paper and produced in a sustainable manner.

Contents

National Styles in Science, Diplomacy, and Science Diplomacy: a Case Study of the United Nations Security Council P5 Countries   1
> *Olga Krasnyak*

Abstract   1

Keywords   1

Part 1   1

Introduction: Science Diplomacy in the Making   1

1   Outline of the Study   4
- 1.1   *The Problem of National Style in Science Diplomacy*   4
- 1.2   *Methodology*   6
- 1.3   *The Case Study*   7
- 1.4   *Science Diplomacy in Focus*   9

2   Science Diplomacy in a *Realism* Loop   15
- 2.1   *Why Realism?*   15
- 2.2   *Realism in IR Theories and Great Power Behaviour*   19
- 2.3   *Realism in Diplomatic Theories*   24
- 2.4   *Hypotheses of State Behaviour*   27

3   National Style and Global Governance   29
- 3.1   *National Style in Science*   29
- 3.2   *National Style in Diplomacy*   33
- 3.3   *The Universal and the National*   37
- 3.4   *National Style in Science Diplomacy and Global Governance*   38

Part 2   40

4   United Kingdom   41
- 4.1   *Scientific Pragmatism and Ethics*   41
- 4.2   *Diplomacy of Realism and Diplomacy of Possibility*   43
- 4.3   *A Trendsetter in Science Diplomacy*   46

5   France   49
- 5.1   *The Inseparability of the French State and Science*   49
- 5.2   *'Movement' Diplomacy and Diplomacy of 'Cohabitation'*   52
- 5.3   *Scientific and Cultural Diplomacy*   56

6   The United States   58
- 6.1   *American Science*   58
- 6.2   *Forward-deployed Diplomacy*   60
- 6.3   *A Science Diplomacy Leader*   65

VI

7 Russia 68
    7.1   *The Russian Century of Science* 68
    7.2   *Network Diplomacy* 71
    7.3   *Embracing the Potential of Science Diplomacy* 74

8 China 77
    8.1   *A Non-Western Power* 77
    8.2   *Chinese Syncretism* 78
    8.3   *The Toolbox of Diplomacy* 80

Conclusion: Science Diplomacy in Perspective 83

Acknowledgement 90

References 90

National Styles in Science, Diplomacy, and Science Diplomacy: a Case Study of the United Nations Security Council P5 Countries

Olga Krasnyak
Underwood International College, Yonsei University Seoul 03722
Republic of Korea
olga.k@yonsei.ac.kr

Abstract

Science diplomacy is becoming an important tool by which states can more effectively promote and secure their foreign policy agendas. Recognising the role science plays at national and international levels and identifying a state's national diplomatic style can help to construct a 'national style' in science diplomacy. In turn, understanding science diplomacy can help one evaluate a state's potential for global governance and to address global issues on a systematic scale. By using a Realist framework and by testing proposed hypotheses, this study highlights how different national styles in science diplomacy affect competition between major powers and their shared responsibility for global problems. This study adds to our general understanding of the practice of diplomacy as it intersects with the sciences.

Keywords

science diplomacy – national style – foreign policy – global governance – the United Nations Security Council's five permanent members

Part 1

Introduction: Science Diplomacy in the Making

2017 was the UK-Russia Year of Science and Education. Led by the influential Royal Society and the British Council on the one side, and by the Russian

Ministry of Education and Science and the Russian Foundation for Basic Research on the other, the year saw a convergence of diplomacy and scientific collaboration between the two countries. Among a number of jointly organised events, scientific conferences, and other people-to-people exchanges, several highlights from the year are worth mentioning. These were a roundtable discussion titled 'Contemporary Science Diplomacy: The Experience of Russia and Britain'[1] held at Moscow's State Institute of International Relations (MGIMO), and the announcement that the UK's Antimicrobial Resistance Centre and Russia's Skolkovo Innovation Centre would join forces against antimicrobial resistance and superbugs.[2] The status and competence of the participants in both featured events have shown the seriousness of both the UK and Russia in developing bilateral relations to implement science-based policy – also known as 'science diplomacy'.

Two questions arise. First, can these particular interstate relations be looked at primarily through the lens of science diplomacy? Second, how do these joint scientific projects differ from regular scientific cooperation that occurs without diplomatic assistance? The answer to the first question is 'yes': it is science diplomacy which is intended to normalise strained relations between the two countries through scientific exchanges, with a view that joint scientific effort might also help to address global issues. The involvement of scientists and other non-state actors in the policy-making process is a critical component of science diplomacy. The answer to the second question revolves around the presence of direct diplomatic assistance in choosing the areas for scientific cooperation between the UK and Russia – cooperation which contributes to securing and promoting the foreign policy objectives of both countries.

The UK-Russia Year of Science and Education shows a few dimensions of science diplomacy: (1) securing foreign policy objectives while improving bilateral relations; (2) enhancing scientific collaboration to address such global issues as antimicrobial resistance and superbugs; (3) generating soft power via people-to-people exchanges and promoting foreign policy objectives through influence, attraction, and cooperation.[3]

---

1 'Royal Society co-Hosts Science Diplomacy Roundtable in Moscow,' *The Royal Society*, 12 May 2017. Available at: https://royalsociety.org/news/2017/05/royal-society-co-hosts-science-diplomacy-roundtable-in-moscow/. Accessed 23 June 2018.

2 'UK and Russian researchers join forces against AMR,' *AMR Centre*, 14 December 2017. Available at: https://www.amrcentre.com/uk-and-russian-researchers-join-forces-against-amr/. Accessed 23 June 2018.

3 Pierre-Bruno Ruffini, *Science and Diplomacy: A New Dimension of International Relations* (Berlin: Springer, 2017), p. 33.

However, despite the success of the 2017 Year of Science and Education, 2018 has seen the deterioration of relations between the UK and Russia. The year has been marked by diplomatic tension and mutual diplomatic closures and expulsions, ultimately putting previous achievements and the potential for further scientific collaboration at risk. At the same time, joint scientific efforts and people-to-people exchanges are looking set to continue, with a hope to rebuild damaged bilateral relations and improve the image of each state in the eyes of the other.

The example of science diplomacy provides a different perspective to the bilateral relationship. The UK is leading the way when it comes to modern science diplomacy in strategy, tactics, and implementation. The UK's advanced scientific endeavours and its large network of embassies and high commissions overseas are actively used for international scientific partnerships and to promote British scientific prowess worldwide. With diplomatic assistance, British scientists are able to mobilise and coordinate international scientific action on specific cross-border issues that are of strategic significance to the UK. When it came to choosing a target for the UK's science diplomacy efforts, Russia was by no means not a random partner. Russia's historical scientific achievements, together with its current status as a (re)emerging scientific power and a regional power, were likely considered to be significant by UK policymakers, and thus of interest for the UK's science diplomacy initiatives. However, the scientific relationship is by no means equal: Russia is a contributing recipient and the UK is an initiator and coordinator in such relations. The UK acts to influence its geopolitical position as a scientifically advanced great power, while Russia uses this cooperation to catch up with scientific progress, keep afloat, and attempt to regain its lost geopolitical influence in the post-Cold War era.

To understand how the UK and Russia play different international roles, this study seeks to understand their differing 'national styles' in science and diplomacy – styles that are derived from community standards, historical and cultural backgrounds, and institutional structures. Recognising elements of national style in science diplomacy helps to identify a state's geopolitical motivations, its diplomatic and strategic behaviour towards other states, and its capacity to negotiate collaborative governance. A state's national style in science diplomacy also bears on its ability to address long-term global challenges and foresee the consequences of such issues as climate change and international inequality.

This study provides a foundation for addressing central questions that ultimately pave the way for further investigation of science diplomacy:
– *Are national styles in science and diplomacy connected?*
– *Are there distinct national styles in science diplomacy?*

– *What are the constructive elements in national styles of science diplomacy and what are their implications for international relations?*

The aim of this study is to explore national style in science diplomacy by analysing historical and cultural circumstances in which national styles have been formed. To do this, I first unpack the concept of science diplomacy. I next bring in a theoretical background in international relations (IR) and diplomacy theory by situating science diplomacy in the tradition of Realism. I then suggest two hypotheses of state behaviour to contextualise science diplomacy perspectives for global governance. I discuss the concept of national style in science and diplomacy before turning to the case study of the United Nations Security Council's five permanent members (the UNSC P5 Countries) – the UK, France, the US, Russia, and China. I then highlight constructive elements of national style in science, diplomacy, and science diplomacy. I tie this analysis together within the empirical cases and provide additional commentary. Expanding on the specifics and limitations of each P5 Country, I suggest that the same methodology might be reasonably applied to examine other powers, both major and minor.

1   Outline of the Study

1.1   *The Problem of National Style in Science Diplomacy*

The concept of national styles in science diplomacy has attracted scant attention by researchers for obvious reasons: science diplomacy itself began a concept in foreign policy affairs only recently, even though science diplomacy has been practiced extensively throughout history.[4] Reconsidering and reimagining various national diplomatic styles is a justifiable way to provide analytical insight into a state's foreign policy.[5] A similar idea can be applied to science diplomacy: recognising particular national styles help us better understand a state's ability to secure and promote its foreign policy objectives using a toolbox of science diplomacy.

The growth of science diplomacy is a critical part of complex international negotiations addressing security dilemmas, estimating the risk of great power conflicts and assessing nuclear threats. Science diplomacy objectives

---

4 Luk Van Langenhove & Elke Boers, 'Science Diplomacy in search of a purpose in the populist era,' *United Nations University Institute on Comparative Regional Integration Studies (UNU-CRIS)*, Issue 2018/4 (March 2018).

5 Jeffrey Robertson, *Diplomatic Style and Foreign Policy: A Case Study of South Korea* (London and New York: Routledge, 2016).

are generally ambitious: they seek to foster global governance that would allow states to collectively examine national or planetary problems, share global responsibility, find common moral ground upon which to build healthy interstate relations, and, ideally, think about the universal good.[6] There is a long tradition within the scientific community of encouraging governments, patrons, and citizens to enlist scientific expertise in the service of the public good.[7] Science diplomacy objectives are oriented to promoting value-creating behaviour – an exchange of concessions and honest information in the pursuit of mutual benefits.

Amid geopolitical rivalries and controversies, science diplomacy is a central element in organising international scientific collaboration addressing global problems, including poverty and starvation, human displacement and statelessness, antimicrobial resistance, earthquakes, volcanic eruptions, climate change, and other natural catastrophes. For such problems, there is an urgent need for diplomatic assistance that can rise above geopolitical controversies. Science diplomacy also potentially provides a sophisticated mechanism to regulate and implement future scientific breakthroughs. For instance, the governance of outer space will inevitably become a global issue as scientific advances lead to greater exploration and commercialisation of the final frontier.[8] Lastly, an increasingly important component of science diplomacy is a state's ability to generate soft power. Considering all these dimensions of science diplomacy, recognising how countries have different national styles in science diplomacy is crucial to understanding the ways in which a state's foreign policy is made and implemented.

In summary, despite the widespread acceptance of the universalism of science and the role of diplomacy as a vital international institution, there are distinct national styles in both science and diplomacy that are derived from differing community standards, historical and cultural backgrounds, and institutional structures. Being cognizant of the history of science and diplomacy allows academics and policymakers to project the future of cooperation between scientists and diplomats. This in turn can help science and diplomacy make joint progress in long-term thinking about the future of global governance.

---

6 Peter Singer, *Ethics in the Real World: 82 Brief Essays on Things That Matter* (Princeton University Press, 2016), p. 262.

7 Mary Jo Nye, 'What price politics? Scientists and political controversy,' *Endeavour*, vol. 23, no. 4 (1999), pp. 148-154.

8 Olga Krasnyak, 'Science Diplomacy: An Underestimated Toolkit of South Korea's Foreign Policy,' *On Korea: Academic Paper Series 2018, Korea Economic Institute of America* (12 April 2018), p. 4.

1.2   *Methodology*

I use a political science methodology to identify great powers' international behaviour. I rely on the use of Realist theory in IR and diplomacy to identify distinguishing features of a state's behaviour when it comes to science diplomacy. This is where the universalism of science and interest-driven great power politics intersect. The result is consistent with common assumptions about the assertive behaviour of great powers in pursuit of their foreign policy objectives, although shows that great powers also recognise ethical considerations and the need to take responsibility for global issues.

This methodology requires a specific strategy. The concept of style in science and diplomacy is examined through the perspective of a country's scientific development and distinct diplomatic traditions and practices. By considering the way in which modern science has been implemented and by underlining the historical and contemporary context in which diplomatic style has been formed and continuously evolved, I outline the concept of national style as it is attempted in science diplomacy in Part 2 of this study.

A country's national style in science diplomacy can be found through combining the recognised elements of its diplomatic style with its way of doing science on a national level. Its diplomatic style can be identified by examining its diplomatic traditions and considering its national and regional characteristics. The same can be achieved for analysing the country's approach to science: acknowledging its scientific way of thinking through a mosaic of historical developments and path dependencies. However, no category is absolute – national styles, whether in diplomacy or science, are evolving and showcasing elements of universality while simultaneously preserving distinct national components. In other words, when national interests constrain a state's ability to negotiate, the universal components of science and diplomacy are used. There are national diplomatic styles and national scientific styles that can be used to evaluate a state's capacity to get what it wants. They can also help us understand the true nature of a state's behaviour, rather than to merely see the shell of a universal diplomatic culture that may say little about a state's real intentions.

Outlining the concept of national style in science diplomacy in a Realist tradition brings us even further – towards deeper comprehension of the phenomena of international influence that is not only based on hard power but also a state's ability to foster attraction and admiration. Put simply, strong science that is developed by a highly advanced great power not only pushes other powers to compete, but also urges them to collaborate with, learn from, and mutually enrich each other. This sort of interstate collaboration and socialisation paves the way to my proposed general hypothesis that evaluating a

NATIONAL STYLES IN SCIENCE, DIPLOMACY, AND SCIENCE DIPLOMACY 7

state's behaviour in science diplomacy is a way to test its aspiration to global governance.

1.3 *The Case Study*

The United Nations Security Council, to which this case study is devoted, was envisioned as the most powerful body in the UN system, consistent with its primary responsibility to maintain world peace based on the principle of collective security. Military strength, economic capability, a broad diplomatic network, and a willingness to promote universal principles and share responsibility, are all perceived to be main characteristics of the P5 Countries – the United Kingdom, France, the United States, Russia, and China.

However, in practice, the UNSC is also one of the most heavily criticised international institutions. This is largely due to the differences between the ideological models and geopolitical visions of its five members and their willingness at times to act with little concern for the values upheld by the UN. Security threats, such as the proliferation of weapons of mass destruction and climate change, could be viewed differently by different members, which leads to the disjointed use of the veto power by the permanent members of the Council. For global stability, peace and security, overcoming the danger of disagreement within the Council ought to be the main task practised by its members.

The use a veto right might be harmful in building long-standing coalitions of like-minded states in the UN General Assembly to achieve the goals of international politics. The power of veto provides to each member an effective means of restraining any other power or spoiling other coalitions and their joint initiatives.

However, the reality is often quite different to the picture just painted. The criticism towards the UNSC is justifiable when disagreement among the P5 Countries is destabilising, for instance, when the US and its NATO allies threaten to confront Russia's military capability. There is also an implicit Western coalition of the US, the UK, France, and Russia confronting the rising power of China. In other analyses, Russia's controversial image and its posture on the international stage is leading the country to strengthen its strategic alliance with China, considering the security dilemma in Russia's Siberia and Far East. Diplomatic tension within both the US-Russia and the UK-Russia relationships are harmful for world stability and increase disagreements within the Council. Other issues as Brexit, the inconsistency of the US foreign policy under the Trump administration, France's attempts to regain its positions in South Pacific, Russia's ongoing involvement in military operations in Ukraine and Syria, and China's geopolitical ambitions in the South and the East China

Seas and Taiwan,[9] are destabilising the world order. These tensions may also be taken as elements in the making of the new geopolitical order with the re-emergence of non-Western powers such as China.

While the economic or military capability of a nation can be measured in numbers of GDP, personnel, munition production, military bases, and so on, it is much harder to calculate the impact of community values and attractiveness. But understanding how states and their policies can be attractive to others, whether intentionally or unintentionally, is necessary to assess how a country generate soft power. Science itself is an element of soft power and a measuring tool in international politics. The idea of a balance of power is the result of long-standing progress in the sciences. The concept traces back to a 19th century article published in the Edinburg Review in 1802,[10] which argues that the power of influence can be measured by a state's scientific development and technological capability – the latter of which is often equivalent to economic growth and military capacity. The P5 Countries are major players in the international system, and their multidimensional approaches in geopolitics require us to consider all the ways in which they wield influence, including soft power.

A state's scientific attractiveness is one of the essential features of science diplomacy soft power. According to the Soft Power 30 annual index,[11] the UK, France, and the US are the leaders in the ranking while Russia and China are far below. Successful countries in soft power are more active in science diplomacy. Of course, science diplomacy alone cannot be an indication of soft power attraction, but science itself is an element of power while the efficiency of diplomatic interactions and networks is another element of soft power.[12]

There is the need to look carefully at the P5 Countries' ability to juggle science and diplomacy individually to better understand how the use of science diplomacy secures and promotes their foreign policy agendas and helps them generate soft power. The P5 Countries have significant influence and are assumed to be great powers, hence a major disagreement or a flashpoint between them might have a disastrous impact on world affairs.

---

9   Brendan Taylor, *The Four Flashpoints: How Asia Goes to War* (Australia: La Trobe University Press, 2018), Kindle Location 134.

10   Herbert Butterfield, 'The Balance of Power' in Herbert Butterfield and Martin Wigh (ed.), *Diplomatic Investigations. Essays in the Theory of International Politics* (Cambridge, Massachusetts: Harvard University Press, 1966), p. 141.

11   More on the website https://softpower30.com.

12   Paul Sharp, *Diplomatic Theory of International Relations* (Cambridge University Press, 2009), p. 56.

1.4   *Science Diplomacy in Focus*

Scientific knowledge has a long history of being utilised in countries' domestic and foreign policies, by both scientifically advantaged countries and by those who lack of scientific innovation. Science is a tool and a bargaining chip in the game of politics. In the following decades, policymakers and foreign policy communities will continue to deal with global issues that are influenced by scientific progress. Countries' domestic and foreign policies and their practices of diplomacy are undergoing a fundamental transformation.

The use of traditional diplomatic assistance for science has normally happened in those cases when diplomatic direct intervention is pivotal and might be the only way to avoid direct confrontation between nations when their relationships are limited or strained. From technical support in issuing visas for scientists from 'problematic' nations (e.g. Cuba and Iran), to international negotiations on scientific collaboration and global regulation, these issues stereotypically associated with diplomatic work. The dramatic transformation of modern diplomacy is caused not only by complexity of negotiations in international politics, but also by the inclusion of specific technical issues to be discussed when diplomats are in urgent need of scientific advice. Thus, the evolution and transformation of traditional diplomacy gave rise to nontraditional diplomacy – science diplomacy – which is becoming an immensely influential mechanism in interstate relations.

The 1961 Vienna Convention on Diplomatic Relations (VCDR) conceptualised the foundation of international diplomatic and consular law. The result was a broad subject area of extensive range of tasks including promoting scientific relations and ascertaining conditions and developments in scientific life between the sending and receiving states.[13] In 2010, the AAAS and the Royal Society issued a report on science diplomacy outlining how it can be used to push a state's foreign policy agenda.[14] This report, together with the establishment of the Center for Science Diplomacy[15] under the umbrella of the AAAS, can be considered an official start for a new discipline. Since 2012, the Center

---

13   Art. 3, 1. (e) of the VCDR. Report of the International Law Commission on the work of its Thirteenth Session, 1 May to July 1961, Official Records of the General Assembly, Sixteenth Session, Supplement No. 10. Extract from the Yearbook of the International Law Commission: 1961, vol. II. Retrieved: http://legal.un.org/ilc/documentation/english/reports/a_cn4_141.pdf. (Accessed 4 June 2018).

14   The AAAS & The Royal Society, 'New frontiers in science diplomacy' (2010).

15   Proclaimed mission of the Center is "to build bridges between communities, societies, and nations through closer interactions between science and diplomacy and elevate the role of science in foreign policy to address national and global challenges." More on the website https://www.aaas.org/program/center-science-diplomacy.

for Science Diplomacy's quarterly publication[16] is an up-to-date resource for various articles devoted to the history and practice of science diplomacy.

The oft-cited 2010 report can be considered a taxonomy for science diplomacy. The intersection of science and diplomacy is such that they can be incorporated in a state's foreign policy as: *science in diplomacy* (informing foreign policy objectives with scientific advice), *diplomacy for science* (facilitating international scientific cooperation), and *science for diplomacy* (using science cooperation to improve international relations between countries). As a starting point, this taxonomy is useful in academic and theoretical discussions and helps to identify how science diplomacy is practically implemented. Each proposed direction has distinguishing features, yet they all overlap with one another to ultimately foster positive interstate relations and support international science. The effectiveness of science diplomacy is heavily dependent on a country's scientific capability and skilful diplomacy.

While the amount of literature devoted to the field of science diplomacy is not yet large, it is rapidly expanding. Several recent seminal works explore the interaction of science and diplomacy. Pierre-Bruno Ruffini's[17] book added much value to the field. Ruffini established the main research questions about the relationship between science and diplomacy even as the essence of both contrast one another: the universality, internationality, and neutrality of science on one hand, and the particularities, bias, and national interest-based foreign policy on the other. The author suggests that the science-diplomacy nexus in its various approaches should be considered a 'smart' power, which is up-to-date with Joseph Nye's concept[18] of soft power.

A collective volume on science diplomacy edited by Lloyd S. Davis and Robert G. Patman is a great collection exploring the number of case studies that can be linked to science diplomacy practices.[19] In this volume, science diplomacy is looked at in the context of a disaggregated diplomatic system emerging from the evolution of international relations and consisting of dynamic networks of lawyers, scientific bodies, non-governmental organisations and the media.

Luk Van Langenhove, a prominent scholar of science diplomacy, should be highlighted considering his immense contribution to the field. Van Langenhove

---

16   See more at: http://www.sciencediplomacy.org/issues.

17   Pierre-Bruno Ruffini, *Science and Diplomacy: A New Dimension of International Relations*, (Berlin: Springer, 2017).

18   Joseph Nye, *Soft Power – The Means to Success in World Politics* (New York: PublicAffairs, 2009).

19   Davis Lloyd & Robert G. Patman (ed.) *Science Diplomacy: New Day or False Dawn?* (World Scientific Publishing Company, 2015).

NATIONAL STYLES IN SCIENCE, DIPLOMACY, AND SCIENCE DIPLOMACY 11

conceptualised science diplomacy and argued that the international scientific community, a change agent, can help establish a multilateral governance structure and strengthen the policy-science nexus.[20]

The bulk of related sources on science diplomacy is represented by policy briefs, reports, short editorials and commentaries, working papers, as well as by scholarly publications. Academics, diplomats, and policymakers attempt to evaluate this new phenomenon and its policy implications. Most publications have a focus on science diplomacy activities as national endeavours. For instance, the US leverage in the field is the most significant: Lord and Turekian, Fedoroff, Colglazier, Chalecki[21] encourage the US government to seek independent scientific advice from its science and technology communities on environmental issues, space policy, and bio- and weapons technology. The US attempts to foster science diplomacy with isolated countries such as Iran[22] and Cuba[23] by seeking to (re)establish connections with local scientists, keep an eye on the progress made by Iranians and Cubans in physics and infectious disease, and evaluate their academic and scientific environment. These specific approaches also indicate the US sensitivity towards Iran and Cuba with whom diplomatic relations are limited.

Other countries have their own concerns. Copeland assesses science diplomacy as part of public diplomacy in Canada, arguing that the main priority for science diplomacy should be to contribute to international science policy;[24] Fähnrich provides a scholarly perspective on the collaboration of science and

---

20   Luk Van Langenhove, 'Global Science Diplomacy for Multilateralism 2.0,' *Science & Diplomacy*, vol. 5, no. 3 (December 2016); Luk Van Langenhove & Elke Boers 'Science Diplomacy in Search of a Purpose in the Populist Era,' *UNU-CRIS Policy Brief*, issue 4 (March 2018).

21   Kristin M. Lord and Vaughan C. Turekian, 'Time for a New Era of Science Diplomacy,' *Science, New Series*, vol. 315, no. 5813 (9 February, 2007), pp. 769-770; Nina V. Fedoroff, 'Science Diplomacy in the 21st Century,' *Cell*, 136 (9 January 2009), pp. 9-11; William Colglazier, 'Science and Diplomacy,' *Science*, vol. 335 (17 February 2012), p. 775; Elizabeth L. Chalecki, 'Knowledge in Sheep's Clothing: How Science Informs American Diplomacy,' *Diplomacy & Statecraft*, vol. 19 (2008), pp. 1-19.

22   Warren E. Pickett, Anthony J. Leggett and Paul C. W. Chu, 'Science Diplomacy with Iran,' *Nature Physics*, vol. 10 (July 2014), pp. 465-467.

23   Gerald R. Fink, Alan I. Leshner, and Vaughan C. Turekian, 'Science diplomacy with Cuba,' *Science*, vol. 344, issue 6188 (06 June 2014), p. 1065; Joe Roman, James Kraska, 'Reboot Gitmo for U.S.-Cuba research diplomacy,' *Science*, vol. 351, issue 6279 (18 Mar 2016), pp. 1258-1260; Larry McKinney, 'Continue U.S.-Cuban science diplomacy,' *Science*, vol. 358, issue 6370 (22 Dec 2017), p. 1549.

24   Daryl Copeland, 'Science Diplomacy: What's It All About?' *CEPI-CIPS Policy* Brief 13 (November 2011).

politics in Germany;[25] French science diplomacy is determined by its ability to exercise influence on France's international partners through the spheres of education and culture;[26] Japan's perspective on science and technology diplomacy is looked at through the lens of soft power with underdeveloped countries and in pursuit of opportunities for greater international cooperation with developed countries.[27] Russian science diplomacy is a source of concern for the Russian government as it seeks to restore lost Soviet influence.[28] A case study of six countries, France, Germany, Japan, Switzerland, the UK, and the US,[29] aims to persuade these countries to do business in science diplomacy while promoting national foreign policies.

Science diplomacy is an important strategy of foreign affairs in the European Union (EU). A number of works examine this region. Van Langenhove emphasises the role of the EU in promoting and utilising science diplomacy in foreign policy-making to establish mission-driven networks of state policy-makers, scientists and relevant stakeholders.[30] De San Roman and Schunz also look at how science diplomacy underpins the ability of the market power of Europe to expand the scope of the EU's activities.[31] A study by Rüffin and Schreiterer is devoted to a quantitative analysis of science and technology agreements that were signed between the EU and six countries (France, Germany, Switzerland, the UK, the USA, and Denmark).[32] While the study shows that such documents are increasing, it also raises the question of the documents' effectiveness and

---

25   Birte Fähnrich, 'Science diplomacy: Investigating the perspective of scholars on politics – science collaboration in international affairs,' *Public Understanding of Science* (2015), pp. 1-16.

26   Philippe Lane, *French Scientific and Cultural Diplomacy*, (UK: Liverpool University Press, 2013); Alexei V. Shestopal and Nikolay V. Litvak, 'Science Diplomacy: French Experience,' *MGIMO Review on International Relations*, vol. 5(50) (2016), pp. 106-114. (In Russian).

27   Taizo Yakushiji, 'The Potential of Science and Technology Diplomacy,' *Asia-Pacific Review*, vol. 16 (1) (2009), pp. 1-7.

28   K. A. Ibragimova and O. N. Barabanov, 'About the Prospects of the Russian Science Diplomacy,' *Vestnik RFFI* [Russian Foundation for Basic Research Herald], no 1 (97) (January-March 2018), pp. 57-59.

29   Tim Flink and Ulrich Schreiterer, 'Science diplomacy at the intersection of S&T policies and foreign affairs: toward a typology of national approaches,' *Science and Public Policy*, vol. 37(9) (November 2010), pp. 665-677.

30   Luk Van Langenhove, 'Tools for an EU Science Diplomacy' (Luxembourg: Publications Office of the European Union, 2017).

31   Alea Lopes De San Roman & Simon Schutz, 'Understanding European Union Science Diplomacy,' *Journal of Common Market Studies* (2017), pp. 1-20.

32   Nicolas Rüffin & Ulrich Schreiterer, 'Case Study Science and Technology Agreements in the Toolbox of Science Diplomacy: Effective Instruments or Insignificant Add-ons?' *EL-CSID Working Paper*, issue 2017/6 (September 2017).

NATIONAL STYLES IN SCIENCE, DIPLOMACY, AND SCIENCE DIPLOMACY

science policy implications. Proud investigates the Horizon 2020 project and its extension to international relations and diplomacy.[33] Moedas looks at science diplomacy from the perspective of multilateralism and collective-responsibility and its role in effective European neighbourhood policy.[34] Ibragimova concludes that no state in the world today can cope independently with modern global challenges.[35]

Science diplomacy objectives are reflected in some government documents. For example, science, technology, and innovation are claimed to be essential in Spain's foreign policy.[36] A report issued by the UK Houses of Parliament considered post-Brexit initiatives on science diplomacy,[37] showing that the UK government plans to develop international partnerships well beyond the EU. There is also a report on the US perspective on global science policy and science diplomacy issued by the National Academy of Sciences.[38] This report points out the importance of active engagement of American scientists in global affairs. The role of science diplomacy in the US is also distinguished and stretches across the societal and natural domains, undertaking questions of governance, economics, the promotion of universal values, and how to understand global issues as an ecosystem.

Whether science diplomacy is a part of public diplomacy or a distinct part of traditional diplomacy, there are non-state actors, scientists and scientific communities, NGO and think-tanks, who mediate in diplomatic negotiations. While individual scientists may hesitate or simply do not feel the need to mediate in diplomacy, technological giants and international corporations feel no such restraint and have the ability to influence interstate relations and

---

33   Virginia Proud, 'The Hunt for Science Diplomacy: Practice and Perceptions in the Horizon 2020 Scientific community, *EL-CSID Working Paper*, issue 2018/18 (June 2018).

34   Carlos Moedas, 'Science Diplomacy in the European Union,' *Science & Diplomacy* (March 2016). Available at http://www.sciencediplomacy.org/perspective/2016/science-diplomacy-in-european-union. Accessed 8 August, 2018.

35   K. A. Ibragimova, 'EU Science Diplomacy and Framework Programmes as Instruments of STI Cooperation,' *MGIMO Review on International Relations*, vol. 5(56) (2017), pp. 151-168. (In Russian).

36   'Report on Science, Technology, and Innovation Diplomacy,' Government of Spain (2016); Ana Elorza Moreno, et al. 'Spanish Science Diplomacy: A Global and Collaborative Bottom-Up Approach,' *Science & Diplomacy* (March 2017). Available at: http://www.sciencediplomacy.org/article/2017/spanish-science-diplomacy-global-and-collaborative-bottom-approach. Accessed 8 August, 2018.

37   'Science Diplomacy,' Houses of Parliament, number 568 (February 2018).

38   'U.S. and International Perspectives on Global Science Policy and Science Diplomacy: Report of a Workshop,' National Academy of Sciences (2012).

diplomacy. Pamment[39] develops the 'mediatisation of diplomacy' concept and argues that it alters the epistemological and ontological grounds for representing diplomatic identities and the ways in which diplomatic actors know and experience themselves. In view of science diplomacy's exclusiveness, it might be that this new field will impact traditional diplomacy. Understanding the nature of science diplomacy and its outcomes is a necessity to be considered by academics and practitioners in related fields.

This brief analysis of the existing literature on science diplomacy shows that it is a rapidly expanding area in need of more academic attention. The intersection between science and diplomacy is implied by the potential for state power and scientific development to influence, govern, and prospectively address global issues while sharing global responsibility. This dyad of science and diplomacy puts great powers in a position to compete with each other and, at the same time, to collaborate with one another despite challenging political environments and changing geopolitics.

Science diplomacy is a prospective area of study and policy consideration. Examining how great powers, particularly the P5 Countries, see the nature and role of science diplomacy in modern politics is a starting point to evaluate the weight of these great powers in global policy-making. Such analysis provides insight into states' behaviour and their ability to set the tone in shaping the international order and influencing other states, whether through cohesive or soft power. Put another way, the key questions are:

- *How do the implicit characteristics of a state, both inherited and evolved over time, impact its current explicit behaviour in pursuing influence?* and
- *What is the role for science diplomacy or related historical practices in such behaviour?*

To narrow this perspective, I next investigate how IR and diplomacy theories in the Realist tradition fit in with the study. In outlining the theoretical framework, I attempt to include works made by not only widely-cited scholars belonging to an American social science and the English IR school, but also less referenced French and Russian IR theorists. I also attempt to include Chinese IR scholarly publications should there be a relevant opportunity. I then suggest two hypotheses to test great power behaviour in the lens of science diplomacy.

---

39   James Pamment, 'The Mediatisation of Diplomacy,' *The Hague Journal of Diplomacy*, vol. 9 (2014), pp. 253-280.

NATIONAL STYLES IN SCIENCE, DIPLOMACY, AND SCIENCE DIPLOMACY 15

2 Science Diplomacy in a *Realism* Loop

2.1 *Why Realism?*

To elaborate a theoretical framework, I took inspiration from political scientists theorising and explaining state behaviour from the position of Realism. In an era of ideological divisiveness, social scientists became increasingly sceptical that the institutions of international development could be ideologically neutral.[40] Realism is controversial as it takes a hawkish approach to international relations, and is criticised by Liberalism, Constructivism and other frameworks.

According to classical Realism, diplomacy is used to achieve foreign policy objectives which are constrained by the power of other nations, and to determine which objectives may be compatible with the objectives of other states. Experienced diplomats use a mixture of persuasion, compromise and the threat of force in achieving their states' foreign policy goals. Diplomats, who are adepts at bargaining, use their skills to negotiate in the interests of their countries.[41]

Science diplomacy seeks to inform policy of long-term strategies – a goal which might be problematic amid short political and electoral cycles that usually do not exceed two to seven years.[42] When political and electoral cycles do not work in scientific timeframes, science diplomacy aims to bridge the gap between politics and science. In the long run, the task for diplomats is to bring science to the level of diplomatic negotiation. A state's efficiency at finding solutions in emergencies and formulating science policy depends on many factors, including the country's scientific capacity and its international influence. Thus, how to couple science diplomacy with the Realist focus on building influence and peacefully maintaining the balance of power is a question worthy of academic consideration.

I am also inclined to use agentic theories in IR and diplomacy within the Realist tradition, as these theories evaluate a state's past behaviour, consider its modern system, and attempt to predict a state's future behaviour and through pre-existing conditions.[43] Agentic theories can be applied to diplomatic work which emphasises the power of interpersonal communications to change,

---

40 Jo Guldi & David Armitage, *The History Manifesto* (The UK: Cambridge University Press, 2014), p. 83.

41 Charles E. Ziegler, 'Diplomacy' in Andrei P. Tsygankov (ed.), *Routledge Handbook of Russian Foreign Policy* (New York, NY: Routledge, 2018), p. 124.

42 Jo Guldi & David Armitage, *The History Manifesto*, p. 1.

43 Marcus Holmes, *Face-to-Face Diplomacy. Social Neuroscience and International Relations* (The UK: Cambridge University Press, 2018), p. 12.

transform, or create tensions within the international system. Diplomatic actors – diplomacy and diplomats – operate in an international system in which people form distinct groups and societies yet still seek to interact with one another to serve their national interests. While Realists might undermine diplomatic processes to influence international events, I argue that the tool of science diplomacy can be fairly used by a state to build its international influence. Science diplomacy is also a way to understand the intentions of the others while outlining the moral responsibility of great powers over world affairs. At the same time, it is worth stating that I am not trying to squeeze science diplomacy into Realist framework. I am, however, convinced of the need to use Realism as a framework for science diplomacy.

I start with the main points of Realism. Those can be identified as: "the need for the units to calculate forces, the decisive role of force among the ingredients of power, the permanence of national ambitions and of threats to survival, the imperative of a balance of power, the impossibility of an 'ethics of law' and of peace through law, the wisdom of an ethics of responsibility instead of an ethics of conviction, the importance of geopolitical factors in the definition of states' goals, the preponderant role of states among all the actors on the world stage, and the possibility of conceptualising politics as 'the intelligence of a personified state' rather than as the intelligence of a class, ideology, or complex and indeterminate bureaucratic process."[44] Put another way, Realism considers national states as primary actors in international relations, and state interests to be the source of changes or clashes, so long as the international system has an anarchic nature.[45] Diplomats act in accordance with the logic of the existing anarchical system of power distributed between self-interested, self-helping, power-maximisers.[46] Realism is associated with state-centrism, the concern with national interest, and the commitment to science, when a state's international behaviour and diplomatic communications are rather constituted from a 'top-down' perspective and are revealed to other states through foreign policy and diplomacy.

Paul Sharp, an influential diplomacy theorist, argues that the Realist hegemony was recently overthrown, even though Realism is still an intellectual force in international politics.[47] However, I think it is too early to neglect

---

44   Stanley Hoffmann, 'Raymond Aron and the Theory of International Relations,' *International Studies Quarterly*, vol. 29, no. 1 (March 1985), p. 15.

45   Pierre Hassner, 'Raymond Aron: Too Realistic to Be a Realist?' *Constellations*, vol. 14, no. 4 (2007), pp. 498-505.

46   Paul Sharp, *Diplomatic Theory of International Relations* (The UK: Cambridge University Press, 2009), p. 54.

47   Paul Sharp, *Diplomatic Theory of International Relations*, p. 53.

NATIONAL STYLES IN SCIENCE, DIPLOMACY, AND SCIENCE DIPLOMACY

Realism from international politics, as rapid changes in current interstate relations are making Realism relevant again. Russia's annexation of Crimea, the hybrid military conflict in the Eastern Ukraine, the ongoing war in Syria, Iran's assertive behaviour towards Israel, North Korea's nuclear program, China's military assets in the South China Sea and the wider region – all these examples indicate states' movements to proclaim or gain geopolitical power and urge other powers to react in their own right. Thus, Realism in international politics is still a powerful set of perceptions shaping states' actual behaviour.

The US is no exception from this list, even though the country is deeply liberal. Moreover, in a recent book, prominent political scientist John Mearsheimer argues that liberal hegemony was destined to fail while nationalism and realism will ultimately have more influence on international politics. Mearsheimer suggests that American policymakers should abandon liberal hegemony and pursue a more restrained foreign policy based on realism and a proper understanding of how nationalism constrains great powers.[48] Embarking from this starting point, below I outline a more detailed justification for using Realist theories in IR and diplomacy, preluded with a brief introduction of two other leading ideas: Liberalism and Constructivism. These latter theories, however, seem less relevant for science diplomacy aspirations.

The concept of Liberal IR and diplomacy theory is based on the goal of maintaining perpetual peace through international institutions and organisations while increasing transparency and avoiding uncertainty over other states' intentions. However, in the contemporary world, the rise of the non-Western power of China has reminded us that national strengths relates to the material world and therefore to all of technology and engineering.[49] This requires us to re-evaluate the principles of the liberal order. China can hardly be called a liberal country, as its own cultural values, practices, and histories can be taken as a fundamental threat to the modern international order – an order created by and for the West.[50] In addition, Russia's switch from declared democratic principles following the collapse of the Soviet Union towards autocracy in recent decades[51] is also a challenge for theoretical Liberalism to be fully implemented.

The post-Cold War American-led institutional order is further challenged by the external change in geopolitics as well as internal political polarisation.

---

48 John J. Mearsheimer, *Great Delusion: Liberal Dreams and International Realities* (Yale University Press, 2018), Kindle locations 44-49.

49 Jo Guldi & David Armitage, *The History Manifesto*, p. 55.

50 Christian Reus-Smit, 'Cultural Diversity and International Order,' *International Organisation*, vol. 71 (2017), pp. 851-885.

51 Pierre Hassner, 'Russia's Transition to Autocracy,' *Journal of Democracy*, vol. 19, no. 2 (April 2008), pp. 5-15.

The collective security proposition maintained by the United Nations might also be at risk due to explicit controversies among the P5 Countries with clashing interests and contrasting ideological aspirations. The processes of globalisation and economic interdependence do not necessarily ensure global peace and security. At the same time, current economic sanctions on Russia put in place by the US and the EU are not a stabilising factor when it comes to building healthy interstate relations. Hence, the decline of the liberal institutional order might prove to be one of the greatest challenges to the theory of Liberalism.

The post-Cold War theory of Constructivism is much harder to identify precisely. Based on various social interactions, Constructivism puts ideas, norms, and identity at the core of the state system. Constructivist theories consider ideas and perceptions no less than material forces and state interests. Wendt,[52] one of the main scholars behind constructivist theory, argues that system-level interactions could transform the identities of states that are influenced by both domestic factors and the international system. Wendt attempts to establish a theory of the international system as a social construction that may potentially absorb (neo)realism with its material purposes and (neo)liberalism with its idealistic system.[53] Wendt considers the material aspects of power and of the international system that makes his theory closer to Realism, however.

Realism in IR and diplomacy theories are more likely to take leading positions in explaining the reshaping of the new world order. Agentic theories in the Realist tradition are a feasible base for this study evaluating science diplomacy as a tool in reinforcing great power influence. The Realist tradition represents the world in terms of interests and power, although it is difficult to specify exactly what power is and why interest-driven states want to possess it.[54]

Let's assume that gaining power is a self-interested thing to do, both for the sake of power itself and for other rewards it brings, such as influence, fame, and resources. Thus, the desire for power in world politics might not be strictly for self-interest but for achieving the things a state wants to do on a larger scale. States can do many things if they have power. Gaining power should not necessarily have a negative connotation in political life – nor is pursuing power in world politics necessarily unethical. Gaining power can be a way to embrace ethical concerns in order to make the world a better and fairer place for everyone.

52　Alexander Wendt, *Social Theory of International Politics* (The UK: Cambridge University Press, 1999), p. 21.

53　Ibid., p. 32.

54　Paul Sharp, *Diplomatic Theory of International Relations*, p. 53.

NATIONAL STYLES IN SCIENCE, DIPLOMACY, AND SCIENCE DIPLOMACY   19

The opposite is applicable as well – the more responsibility a state holds, the more tragic the consequences of making the wrong decision.[55] One may say that moral responsibility is incurred by creating a situation in which global problems arise. For example, smaller powers by themselves could not possibly shoulder the burden of climate change due to their own need for industrialisation and economic growth. In this sense, it is the wealthier countries who are responsible and should cover the costs of addressing climate change, and this is perceived to be a price for global influence.

As previously mentioned, power is hard to define. Whether from a psychological perspective or using qualitative characteristics of a state's performance, certain characteristics can help identify when a state is viewed as a great power on the international stage. Great powers are characterised with decisive behaviour, military capability that includes nuclear and missile capacity, and active foreign policy and diplomacy. These characteristics apply to all P5 Countries. At the same time, great power capacity involves not just sabre-rattling but is also backed up by skilful diplomacy with a broadly expanding diplomatic network, advanced level of scientific and technological development and further potential for such development. The confident and at times provocative behaviour of great powers, their ambitious foreign policies, and the ethics of responsibility, are considered to be characteristics usually missing by smaller powers.

The burden of great power responsibility also tends to generate the soft power of attraction while encouraging smaller powers to cooperate. The duality of such behaviour – to influence and take responsibility – is posed by structural accounts and reflects Realist traditions in IR and diplomacy. In this sense, science diplomacy might surely be considered a long-term strategy with effective tactics and a highly sophisticated toolbox in global foreign policy-making to shape the postures and behaviour of great powers.

2.2   *Realism in IR Theories and Great Power Behaviour*

Realist theory is well defined and widely discussed by distinguished scholars of IR and diplomacy. As diplomatic studies are traditionally seen as secondary to international relations studies, I start with IR theorists and focus on their propositions and linkages to foreign policy-making, diplomacy, and international morality. Then I look at theorists of diplomacy with a focus on how the Realist tradition in diplomacy can be relevant to this study. Placing diplomatic theories after IR theories is not to undermine the study of diplomacy, but

---

55   Peter Singer, *Ethics in the Real World: 82 Brief Essays on Things That Matter* (The US: Princeton University Press, 2016), p. 304.

rather to show its growing importance as part of a renaissance of diplomacy.[56] Finally, I suggest two hypotheses for how this theory would predict a state's behaviour.

Realism traces back to Machiavelli[57] who suggested that a state should pursue an uncompromising 'Realism' to increase its power and should employ continuous diplomacy in a strategy of deception. Nicolson's[58] approach to international politics embraces Realist assumptions about the prevalence of power, but also acknowledges the moral dimension of politics. Nicolson argues the great power concept can be asserted over long periods of time while considering a sense of international morality, and writes that diplomacy itself "only becomes moral when it is the servant of overwhelming power".[59] Morgenthau's[60] classical Realism asserts the nature of a scientific man who is himself the source of conflict, yet proves to be a true Realist with the weapon of science. The idea of a moral man and a moral state that can behave morally despite the political system is suggested by Niebuhr,[61] another classic theorist of Realism. Morality is understood in the sense that a man is able to consider interests others than his own in determining problems of conduct. The idea of a moral man or a moral state is rational, and can be stretched into a framework for outlining the moral responsibilities of great powers.

In evaluating states' behaviour, I draw on some classical Realist theorists who would rather see themselves as rational hawks of international politics. Jervis[62] argues that Realism in international politics perceives the continuity of world politics as a constant negotiation that implies a mixture of common and conflicting interests and sees international security through the causes, conduct, and consequences of conflicts. Jervis also says that while the instruments of diplomacy, both standard and innovative, are underestimated in world politics, they are nevertheless adequate for cooperation and may produce deeper

---

56   Marcus Holmes, *Face-to-Face Diplomacy. Social Neuroscience and International Relations*, p. 8.

57   G. R. Berridge, 'Machiavelli,' in G. R. Berridge, Maurice Keens-Soper & T. G. Otte (ed.), *Diplomatic Theory from Machiavelli to Kissinger* (Palgrave 2001), p. 24.

58   T. G. Otte, "Nicolson" in G. R. Berridge, Maurice Keens-Soper & T. G. (ed.), Otte *Diplomatic Theory from Machiavelli to Kissinger*, p. 154.

59   Harold Nicolson, *Diplomacy* (The UK, London: Oxford University Press, 1942), p. 47.

60   Hans J. Morgenthau, *Scientific Man vs. Power Politics* (Great Britain: Latimer House Limited, 1947), p. 189.

61   Reinhold Niebuhr, *Moral Man and Immoral Society: A Study in Ethics and Politics* (New York City, NY: Charles Scribner's Sons, 1932).

62   Robert Jervis, 'Realism, Neoliberalism, and Cooperation: Understanding the Debate in Colin Elman & Miriam Fendius Elman (ed.), *Progress in International Relations Theory. Appraising the Field* (The US: MIT Press 2003), p. 283.

changes in what actors want and how they conceive of their interests.[63] Jervis's reference to 'innovative' diplomacy leaves ample room for great powers to pursue science diplomacy while gaining influence and taking moral responsibility for global change.

Mearsheimer[64] develops offensive Realism theory by discussing how great powers behave towards one another, noting that they often look for opportunities to gain power at each others' expense. Mearsheimer's theory evaluates the assertive behaviour of great powers in historical context and assumes the possibility for further predictions. Offensive Realism theory sees diplomacy as an instrument of maintaining the balance of power.[65]

In Waltz's[66] view, the other side of a state's behaviour is power derived from the material base of the system. Waltz constructs defensive or structural Realism theory and claims that the outcomes of a state's behaviour are determined by its desire to survive and seek security. By pursuing these goals, states will engage in balancing behaviour whether or not a balance of power is the end of their acts.

French IR theorist Aron,[67] who created an autonomous discipline of international relations, proclaims political Realism as a leading force in French policy-making. He called to an end for "idealist aspirations" in French foreign policy in the 1930s and insisted that disarmament and negotiation could no longer be a substitute for defence.[68] Aron attempts to combine Liberal and Realist insights to understand the international politics of the Old World.[69] Aron also asserts that the "diplomatic strategic behaviour" of great powers can range from survival, to power, glory, or the spread of ideas.[70]

The number of contemporary researchers in Neorealist (alternatively, Structural Realist) traditions and hypotheses is expanding. I here touch upon a few works as they represent great power behaviour. From a historical

---

63   Ibid., pp. 306-307.

64   John J. Mearsheimer, *The Tragedy of Great Power Politics* (New York: W. W. Norton, 2014), eBook.

65   Ibid.

66   Kenneth Walzt, *Theory in International Politics* (Addison-Wesley, 1979), p. 128.

67   Stanley Hoffmann, 'Raymond Aron and the Theory of International Relations,' *International Studies Quarterly*, vol. 29, no. 1 (March 1985), pp. 13-27.

68   Quoted in: Tony Just, *The Burden of Responsibility. Blum, Camus, Aron, and the French Twentieth Century* (Chicago and London: The University of Chicago Press, 1998), p. 132.

69   Raymond Aron, *Peace and War: A Theory of International Relations* (New Brunswick, New Jersey: Transaction Publishers, 2003), p. 3.

70   Pierre Hassner, 'Raymond Aron: Too Realistic to Be a Realist? *Constellations*, vol. 14, no. 4 (2007), pp. 498-505.

perspective, Kagan considers great power behaviour under the Concert of Europe[71] to be in full accord with Realist expectations and concludes that the security issue was not removed from short-term self-interest. In examining the suite of national interests that currently prevent the European Union from making a centralised supranational authority, Grieco[72] uses a Neorealist framework. He identifies nationalism, fears of cheating, dependency, and relative gains as factors that limit the development of the European transnational identity and strengthen national identity and state interest. Lundborg[73] evaluates the international ethics of Neorealism as the structural conditions of a state's survival that make international life possible. Gunitsky,[74] however, looks at the change in theory of structural Realism in explaining that state behaviour leans towards democratic diffusion while ignoring anarchy, integrating Realist theory with Liberalism.

Realists believe that globalisation has little impact in the international arena and that sovereign states are main architects of the phenomenon. They argue that globalisation itself depends on state acquiescence and support.[75] Globalisation has elevated the function of governance, which is defined as multilateral cooperation to solve collective action problems in a way that gives equal importance to everyone involved.[76] In this sense, interest-driven great powers orchestrate the world order by relying on globalisation for beneficial economic cooperation and as a way to promote their foreign policy objectives. Supranational gatherings such as the World Trade Organization (WTO), World Bank, G-20, G-8, and G-7, are intended to extend credit, trade, and entrepreneurship worldwide and provide a cure for any society's economic ills.[77] The latest round of globalisation has seen the intensification and acceleration of the reshaping of political cognition. In political cognition, great powers facili-

---

71   Korina Kagan, 'The Myth of the European Concert: The Realist-Institutionalist Debate and Great Power Behaviour in the Eastern Question, 1821-41,' *Security Studies*, vol. 7, no. 2 (1997), pp. 1-57.

72   Joseph M. Grieco, 'The Maastricht Treaty, Economic and Monetary Union and the Neo-Realist Research Programme,' *Review of International Studies*, vol. 21, no. 1 (January 1995), pp. 21-40.

73   Tom Lundborg, 'The ethics of neoRealism: Waltz and the time of international life,' *European Journal of International Relations* (2018).

74   Seva Gunitsky, 'Complexity and Theories of Change in International Politics,' *International Theory*, vol. 5, no. 1 (2013), pp. 35-63.

75   David Held, Anthony McGrew, David Goldblatt & Jonathan Perraton, *Global Transformations: Politics, Economics, and Culture* (Stanford University Press, 1999), p. 10.

76   Ole Jacob Sending, Vincent Pouliot & Iver B. Neumann, 'The Future of Diplomacy,' *International Journal*, vol. 66, no. 3 (2011), pp. 527-542.

77   Jo Guldi and David Armitage, *The History Manifesto*, p. 73.

NATIONAL STYLES IN SCIENCE, DIPLOMACY, AND SCIENCE DIPLOMACY 23

tate protocols and implement various regulations internationally[78] primarily enhances their own influence.

Among Russian IR theorists, Realism is a dominant theory and a leading intellectual movement. Realism reflects the symbiosis of two entities: a political and value-oriented approach on the one hand, and national interest on the other. Realism justifies Russia's international behaviour.[79] Russia's Realist school views the world order as the configuration of great powers and their attempts to spread and manage spheres of influence globally, underlining the external factors of Russia's place on the international stage rather than focusing on internal issues.[80] Russia pursues its place as a great power by starting from its large geographical spread eastwards and building its sole regional dominance, then attempting to step up towards the multi-polar world and partaking in global governance.[81]

Andrei Tsygankov, a prominent IR theorist, argues that the Russian school in IR theory is compatible to that of the English IR school, and should be recognised equally. Tsygankov does not attempt to squeeze Western IR theories into Russia's view of international relations, but rather suggests theoretical foundations for an exclusive Russian IR school of thought.[82]

As most scholars agree, IR theory is a relatively new academic subject in China. The field has been thriving since the 'learning-copying' period of the 1980s, which was then followed by the 'stimulus-respond' period and is now finally moving towards the 'reflecting-constructing' period.[83] It might still be too early to say that the Chinese IR school of thought has been formed. Indeed, Chinese IR theory might be better called a theory of IR with Chinese characteristics. The theory heavily relies on China's traditional respect for Marxism and the official ideology formulated by Chinese leadership. It integrates Chinese

---

78   Jason Dittmer, *Diplomatic Material: Affect, Assemblage, and Foreign Policy* (Duke University Press, 2017), p. 13.

79   Tatyana A Shakleyina & Aleksei D Bogaturov, 'Russian Realist School of International Relations,' *Communist and Post-Communist Studies*, vol. 37, issue 1 (March 2004), pp. 37-51.

80   Dmitry Streltsov & Artem Lukin, 'Russian-Japanese Rapprochement Through the Lens of IR theory. Neo-classical Realism, Constructivism, and Two Level Games,' *International Trends*, vol. 15, no. 2 (April-June 2017), pp. 44-63, (in Russian).

81   Marina M. Lebedeva & Maxim V. Kharkevich, 'Theory of International Relations in the Mirror of Contemporary Russian International Studies,' *MGIMO Review on International Relations*, vol. 5(50) (2016), pp. 7-19, (in Russian).

82   Andrei Tsygankov, *The Russian International Theory: The Three Traditions* (Russia, Moscow: RuScience 2018), (in Russian).

83   Yiwei Wang, 'China. Between copying and constructing' in Arlene B. Tickner & Ole Wæver (ed.), *International Relations. Scholarship Around the World* (New York, NY: Routledge, 2009), pp. 103-119.

civilisational, cultural, and traditional values on the one hand with a thorough study of Western IR theories on the other.[84]

Notably, the meaning of the word 'theory' in China differs from the West. 'Theory' from the Western perspective is something that explains and predicts, while the Chinese understanding of 'theory' is constituted out of the concepts of socialist revolution and construction that are ultimate adaptations of Marxism and Leninism.[85] Classical Realism, Liberalism, and Constructivism have been introduced into China and became the dominant discourse within the Chinese IR theory. In this space, Realism is considered either as a model to be learned or rejected, and Chinese scholars consequently have a love-hate relationship with it.[86] Realism clearly emphasises national power and has become the first established Western IR theory in the Chinese IR community. It continues to be one of the most influential traditions in Chinese political science.[87]

2.3 *Realism in Diplomatic Theories*

Until a decade ago, there was little theoretical interest in diplomacy. Before analysing diplomatic theories, I draw on ideas developed by Marcus Holmes when constructing a theory of face-to-face diplomacy. Holmes writes that diplomacy and diplomatic theory should not be shoehorned into IR theories or viewed as alternative to structure. Instead, the work of diplomats creates structure itself. Diplomacy is about structuring, he argues, rather than working against structures.[88]

In comparison with IR theories, there are relatively few scholarly efforts to conceptualise a diplomatic theory of international relations. This is understandable, as diplomatic work reflects a state's position towards other states. Consequently, diplomacy and how states go about communicating and pursuing their interests through diplomatic work follows international relations. Diplomacy, for its part, tests states' ability to successfully negotiate agreements.

---

84 Gerald Chan, *Chinese Perspectives on International Relations. A Framework for Analysis* (Palgrave Macmillan, 1999), pp. 140-143; Yan Xuetong, 'Chinese Values vs. Liberalism: What Ideology Will Shape the International Normative Order?' *The Chinese Journal of International Politics*, (2018), pp. 1-22.

85 Gustaaf Geeraerts & Men Jing, 'International Relations Theory in China,' *Global Society*, vol. 15, no. 3 (2001), pp. 251-276.

86 Gerald Chan, *Chinese Perspectives on International Relations. A Framework for Analysis*, p. 166.

87 Yaqing Qin, 'Development of International Relations Theory in China: Progress Through Debates,' *International Relations of the Asia-Pacific*, vol. 11 (2011), pp. 231-257.

88 Marcus Holmes, *Face-to-Face Diplomacy. Social Neuroscience and International Relations*, p. 11.

NATIONAL STYLES IN SCIENCE, DIPLOMACY, AND SCIENCE DIPLOMACY

Diplomats, as agents of their nation-states, pursue foreign policy agendas through interpersonal communication and presumably skilfully manage the material body of diplomatic interactions via assemblages, inferences, and personal encounters. Diplomatic work can and should be explained by diplomatic theories when such work is the result of the leading ideas of diplomats who have themselves studied diplomacy.[89] Diplomatic theory may be viewed as a result of integrating social theory and international relations theory. There are several traditions of diplomatic theory which can be distinguished in scholarly publications.

Paul Sharp, who is in the forefront of constructing diplomatic theory, extracts three traditions of international thought in diplomacy: radical, rational, and Realist.[90] The Realist tradition in diplomacy is always strong, as states often say they want power and rely on the power of interpersonal relations. Realism is the focus when a state's capacity is more advanced compared to others in the system, and diplomacy and diplomats may be viewed as another element of power.[91] Sharp notes that Realism in diplomacy not only seeks material explanations, but also contains ideational elements derived from human nature, psychology, and interpersonal interactions. These elements can affect the extent to which great powers can influence smaller powers and their willingness to establish international institutions for global governance and cooperation. If diplomacy under a Realist approach is a tool for global governance, this does indeed represent a threat to traditional diplomacy, due to the variety of actors that enter the international arena.[92] These premises of diplomatic theory in the Realist tradition are suitable to fit science diplomacy as a tool to explain the behaviour of great powers. Diplomats act as architects in the construction of more civilised conditions for the conduct of international relations.[93]

Rather than constructing diplomatic theory, Bjola and Kornprobst conducted substantive analysis of social theories that can be applied to diplomacy. For instance, social theories that integrate different disciplines – psychology and sociology – evaluate human behaviour and the methodology of making decisions. Understanding psychology in interpersonal interactions is highly

---

89 Paul Sharp, *Diplomatic Theory of International Relations*, p. 6.

90 Ibid.

91 Ibid., p. 56.

92 Christer Jönsson, 'Global Governance: Challenges to Diplomatic Communication, Representation, and Recognition' in Andrew F. Cooper, Brian Hocking & William Maley (ed.), *Global Governance and Diplomacy. Worlds Apart?* (The UK: Palgrave Macmillan, 2008), p. 30.

93 Paul Sharp, *Diplomatic Theory of International Relations*, p. 43.

relevant to the communication-making process, which is one of the primary skills of diplomats. More specifically, game theory evaluates the strategic interactions through which diplomats, the actors of international politics, make decisions.[94] Deontological theory explains the diplomatic construction of the world, how moral values are shaped, and our responsibilities for treating one another respectfully.[95] As for the schools of thought, Bjola and Kornprobst use a classical approach which is also relevant to IR theories – Realism, Liberalism, and Constructivism. The spectrum of Realism approaches is delimited by the concept of 'outlaws' on the one hand and 'allies' on the other. Interstate relations evolve according to the structural pressures to guard the security of a state in an anarchical environment.[96]

Berridge et al.[97] look at diplomatic theory through the lens of diplomatic classics. Their book includes a collection of selected authors of diplomacy and aims to stimulate interest in diplomatic theory rather than to merely outline it. However, in a book[98] devoted to the theory and practice of diplomacy, Berridge does not define diplomatic theory except through a reference to 'functional theory', which denotes practices of diplomacy involving the persuasive justification of diplomatic privileges and immunities for the proper functioning of diplomatic missions.

Rathbun[99] builds a theory of diplomacy, looking for guidance in three areas of psychological literature – negotiation, political ideology, and moral values – and ends up with a theory of diplomacy as agency. Regarding Realism, Rathbun uses a theoretical outline to deal with a diplomatic style he called 'pragmatic statecraft.' This diplomatic style focuses on securing vital interests while conceding others, is oriented toward the long term, emphasises the importance of cold and objective decision-making, is adaptive to a state's particular environment, and uses appropriate tools for the time. These characteristics sound like a working combination to achieve science diplomacy objectives.

Holmes and Rofe[100] distinguish theory in diplomacy according to a dichotomy between Liberalism/pluralism and Realism, and write that both

94   Corneliu Bjola & Markus Kornprobst, *Understanding International Diplomacy. Theory, practice and ethics* (New York, NY: Routledge, 2013), p. 82.

95   Ibid., p. 132.

96   Ibid., p. 129.

97   G. R. Berridge, Maurice Keens-Soper & T. G. Otte (ed.), *Diplomatic Theory from Machiavelli to Kissinger* (Basingstoke: Palgrave, 2001).

98   G. R. Berridge, *Diplomacy. Theory and Practice* (The UK: Palgrave Macmillan, 2010).

99   Brian C. Rathbun, *Diplomacy's Value: Creating Security in 1920s Europe and the Contemporary Middle East* (Ithaca, NY: Cornell University Press, 2014), p. 22.

100   Alison Holmes & J. Simon Rofe, *Global Diplomacy: Theories, Types, and Models* (Boulder, CO: Westview Press, 2016), p. 68.

NATIONAL STYLES IN SCIENCE, DIPLOMACY, AND SCIENCE DIPLOMACY   27

dimensions seem to mutually co-exist. The scholars suggest that Realist approaches in the study of diplomacy is as central as those within the academic discipline of international relations. Realism in diplomatic theory is not static but evolves just as every IR theory does. In addition, the behaviour of great powers and superpowers demonstrates how Realism and Liberalism can both be incorporated into such theoretical frameworks.[101]

In this brief analysis of IR and diplomacy theories, I attempted to outline a theoretical framework for my current study, emphasising the relevance of the Realist tradition. Realism is a viable foundation that helps to understand and further explain the international behaviour of the P5 countries and the prospect for science diplomacy being implemented into their foreign policy. Below I suggest several hypotheses to explain how the essence of science diplomacy can impact great power behaviour.

2.4   *Hypotheses of State Behaviour*

The turn towards a multi-polar world requires great powers to keep up with or revise their positions on the international stage. In other words, an emerging new world order compels the great powers to consider whether their existing international postures can be reinforced, or whether it is necessary to adjust their strategies. Science diplomacy is seen as an important mechanism not only to be implemented into a state's foreign policy agenda, but also as a tool to shape interstate relations. The dyads of science diplomacy – global influence and global responsibility – could be the cornerstone of great power behaviour. Following this logic and relying on Realist assumptions, there are two hypotheses of state behaviour in the context of the use of science diplomacy:

1)   **A great power's assertive behaviour is based on advantageous scientific development** that is predetermined by the state's economic, technological, scientific, and military capability. These assets form its foreign policy agenda in which increasing diplomacy of influence is accessed from positions of hard power of cohesion and persuasion.

2)   **A great power has moral responsibility to address global challenges and promote peaceful resolutions in the face of security dilemmas.** This hypothesis suggests that when a country is advanced and influential, it increases its role in generating the soft power of science diplomacy. It also urges a great power to undertake responsibility for global issues and engage with smaller powers through attraction and cooperation. This position can be driven by a rational and egoistic social force in order to establish social harmony between all human societies and collectives.

---

101   Ibid., p. 69.

Pre-existing conditions impact interstate relations and great power behaviour. However, the existing geopolitical arrangements, such as the power of the state and social institutions, also impact a state's international posture. Such conditions might diminish the historically-formed foundations upon which great powers find inspiration or motives for their behaviour. On the other hand, the existing conditions, when looked at through a Realist lens, pave the way towards gaining more international influence – influence which aims not only to have the state recognised by others as a great power, but also to preserve geopolitical interests, whether through hard power capacity or through a genuine inclination towards attraction and cooperation.

Science gives a huge advantage to states. It is itself a driving force behind a state's power and can be seen as a threat by smaller powers, generating fear and deterrence. To soften this threat, the soft power of science diplomacy is perceived to be no less important than traditional diplomacy in maintaining interstate relations.

I follow common sense in defining great powers through their ability to influence others (stressing the importance of national and, perhaps, even nationalistic interests), pursue universally accepted and meaningful research programs, communicate practical policy advice, and instruct future generations.[102] Protecting one's national interest often goes hand in hand with opposing other states when they might be seen as a threat to a national security. However, declaring the universal good merges the national and the global on a structural level, for such issues as nuclear arms control and sustainable development. Promoting international collaboration and admitting responsibility for global issues is a way for great powers to follow this path. In this sense, science diplomacy is not only a sophisticated mechanism of foreign policy, but also a universal tool to address natural challenges and security dilemmas.

In the next section, I outline the concept of national style in both science and diplomacy, considering its universal, national, and regional components. Such analysis will be a basis for identifying national styles in science diplomacy. I then argue that science diplomacy has the potential to be used for global governance.

---

102 Jeffrey Robertson, 'Middle-power definitions: confusion reigns supreme,' *Australian Journal of International Affairs*, vol. 71, no. 3 (March 2017), pp. 1-16.

3 National Style and Global Governance

3.1 *National Style in Science*

Science is universal, but the ways in which knowledge is produced remain largely national. The existence of national schools such as the Russian school of mathematics, the German school of chemistry, or the French school of sociology continue as important centres of accumulation of intellectual resources.[103] Acknowledging the historical background in which science is represented, and the historical circumstances which influenced a country's diplomatic traditions and practices, is a way to highlight a series of constructive elements of national style.

Mary Jo Nye, a historian of science, explicitly dealt with the concept of national styles in science and argued that cognitive and social styles exist in science, while style determines creativity, community values, and support.[104] These components can equally be used to explain the success or failure of individual, institutional, and national scientific endeavours. Style also plays a role in the emergence and perpetuation of scientific ideas, institutions, and ideologies. Mary Jo Nye suggests a definition of national style in science.[105] A conceptual 'style' is a most challenging set of elements linking a country's traditions to both day-to-day scientific work and new ideas or disciplines, and analysing relationships among conceptual style, social organisation, intellectual micro-environments, and practical commitments of individual scientists. These commitments, for many scientists, have always included the utilitarian goal of making scientific progress for the benefit of humanity.

Defining a country's 'national style' might be challenging. The term 'national' not only refers to a nation-state but to people's behaviour, traditions, and customs. Assuming that the extraction of national characteristics that constitute a national style has been completed, then an analysis of given differences between countries might led to provocative – even dangerous – implications. The notion of 'style' can imply racism, nationalism, and chauvinism.[106] Thus, emphasising the idea of national style incurs the risk of stigmatisation by a modern civil society. In contrast, neglecting national styles when insisting on

---

103 Pierre-Bruno Ruffini, *Science and Diplomacy: A New Dimension of International Relations*, p. 97.

104 Mary Jo Nye, 'National Styles? French and English Chemistry in the Nineteen and Early Twentieth Centuries, *Osiris* 2, no. 8 (1993), pp. 30-49.

105 Mary Jo Nye, 'Recent Sources and Problems in the History of French Science,' *Historical Studies in the Physical Sciences*, vol. 13, no. 2 (1983), p. 414.

106 Mary Jo Nye, 'National Styles? French and English Chemistry in the Nineteen and Early Twentieth Centuries,' pp. 30-49.

other common generalisations would be harmful for understanding interstate relations, and would not help to explain the rise of national movements, such as the recent populist and nationalist backlash against globalisation and the shock of the Brexit and Trump victories.[107]

The use of the concept of national style is not new. It is in fact a well-researched idea in scholarly literature devoted to the history of science, with a main focus on British, French, German, Russian, and American national styles in science.[108] National styles exist, and they are not automatic consequences of a shared biology, genetics, and geography; rather, they are social constructions.[109]

Modern science emerged in the West thanks to pre-existing conditions, in particular European ideas of reason and politics, economics, faith and other aspects of culture.[110] In other words, loosening the connection between science and reason might diminish a country's national scientific endeavours, transform its interstate relations, and weaken the power of its diplomacy. Likewise, maintaining connections between science and reason in different places at different times, and understanding how these connections affect a state's foreign policy and diplomacy, requires a deep exploration of the regional and national history of states. Conceptualising national style in science diplomacy should therefore illuminate the process of international policy-making.

The patterns that underline the possibility for modern science to progress might be common, but specialisations in disciplines are determined by elements rooted in national culture. For example, if chemistry was by and large

---

107   Miles Kahler, 'Global Governance: Three Futures,' *International Studies Review*, vol. 20 (2018), p. 245.

108   Nathan Reingold, 'National Styles in the Sciences: The United States Case,' in E. G. Forbes (ed.), *Human Implications of Scientific Advance* (Edinburgh: Edinburgh Univ. Press, 1978), pp. 163-173; Jonathan Harwood, 'National Styles in Science: Genetics in Germany and the United States between the World Wars,' *Isis*, vol. 78 (1987), pp. 390-414; Anna Wessely, 'Transposing 'Style' from the History of Art to the History of Science,' *Science in Context*, vol. 4 (1991), pp. 265-278; Mary Jo Nye, 'National Styles? French and English Chemistry in the Nineteen and Early Twentieth Centuries,' *Osiris*, vol. 2, no. 8 (1993), pp. 30-49; Mary Jo Nye, 'The Republic vs. The Collective: Two Histories of Collaboration and Competition in Modern Science,' *N.T.M.*, vol. 24 (2016), pp. 169-194; Michael Gordin, Karl Hall & Alexei Kojevnikov (ed.), *Intelligentsia Science: The Russian Century, 1860-1960, Osiris*, Second Series, vol. 23 (Chicago: The University of Chicago Press, 2008); Carol Harrison & Ann Johnson (ed.), *National Identity: The Role of Science and Technology, Osiris*, vol. 24 (2009); Leah Ceccarelli, *On the Frontier of Science: An American Rhetoric of Exploration and Exploitation* (East Lansing, Michigan: Michigan State University, 2013).

109   Mark Walker, 'The 'national' in international and transnational science,' *BJHS*, vol. 45, no. 3 (September 2012), pp. 359-376.

110   Paul Sharp, *Diplomatic Theory of International Relations*, p. 286.

NATIONAL STYLES IN SCIENCE, DIPLOMACY, AND SCIENCE DIPLOMACY 31

a French science, then the natural sciences and comparative anatomy were leading fields in England,[111] and the philosophy of Cosmism and the further rise of space sciences could only appear in Russia.[112] Even within scientific disciplines, national styles can be distinguished: French scientists instilled a tendency toward the theoretical in physical sciences, while English scientists tended toward the experimental.[113] Russian science is commonly called 'intelligentsia science' – the assimilation of science and technology into Russian culture during the 'Russian century' in science.[114] American science is metaphorically associated with the reach to the 'frontiers', portraying American scientists as risk-taking adventurous loners with a manifest destiny to penetrate the unknown, and a competitive desire to make profitable discoveries.[115] While Chinese syncretism did not give rise to modern science, it nevertheless gave the culture an immense ability to make pragmatic adjustments and adaptations.

While different styles in science can be seen at the national level, national style should be distinguished from national science.[116] National science incorporates different cultural norms, economic realities, and social circumstances. The development of national science is affected by research centres, laboratories, funding, and a state's current objectives when "national differences do account for the distinctive icing on pieces of the international cake."[117] The opposite is also true: national science affects the process of nation-state building. Since the Enlightenment, the development of the sciences and engineering has improved people's health and living conditions. Thus, a nation with advanced science and technology is considered more capable and competitive on a global scale.[118]

In the 21st century, the way of doing science became less connected to strictly national endeavours and instead began to adhere to the notion of

111   David Knight, *The Age of Science* (Oxford: Basil Blackwell, 1986), p. 3.

112   Asif A. Siddiqi, 'Imagining the Cosmos: Utopians, Mystics, and the Popular Culture of Spaceflight in Revolutionary Russia,' in Michael Gordin, Karl Hall and Alexei Kojevnikov (ed.), *Intelligentsia Science: The Russian Century, 1860-1960, Osiris*, Second Series, vol. 23 (Chicago: The University of Chicago Press 2008).

113   Mary Jo Nye, 'National Styles? French and English Chemistry in the Nineteen and Early Twentieth Centuries,' pp. 34-37.

114   Michael Gordin, Karl Hall & Alexei Kojevnikov (ed.), *Intelligentsia Science: The Russian Century, 1860-1960.*

115   Leah Ceccarelli, *On the Frontier of Science: An American Rhetoric of Exploration and Exploitation.*

116   Mark Walker, 'The 'national' in international and transnational science'.

117   Quoted in: Mark Walker, 'The 'national' in international and transnational science,' p. 374.

118   Carol Harrison & Ann Johnson, 'Introduction: science and national identity,' pp. 1-14.

promoting the global dissemination of knowledge. This change could signal the end of national science, because science rapidly progresses from the local to the international or transnational.[119] Nation-states develop symbiotic relationships with scientists and scientific institutions both at home and abroad, and do so by negotiating and exchanging things of value for mutual benefit. A single region, locality or culture in a multicultural state can do this too, and indeed certainly sometimes does – but that does not 'prove' that the nation as a concept is obsolete or redundant. While science is clearly both an international and a transnational activity, trying to take the 'national' out of it appears misguided.[120] Walker asked,[121] every other aspect of culture, politics, and society is permeated by the concept of nationality, so why should science be different?

Leaving aside the process of accumulating scientific knowledge throughout human history, when making empirical observations of national style in science diplomacy, I limit my perspective to the modern scientific age. Modern science emerged in the West during the age of science and immensely progressed during the age of global science.[122] These periods do not have strict chronological boundaries and may be called 'ages' or alternatively 'eras.'

The age of science approximately includes the 19th and early 20th centuries. It was a time when the foundations for today's current scientific disciplines were laid and the boundaries between them established – boundaries which turned out to be much more stable than national borders. Derived from David Knight's book of the same title, the 'age of science' is defined as a cumulative enterprise of people of different talents in science-related fields, in competition or coordination with other disciplines, the result of which was the substantial expansion of national state power and the revolutionary transformation of people's lives.[123] The destruction of the two World Wars was not the result of scientific progress, but rather followed the military inertia of previous decades and emerged out of the needs and interests of warring coalitions.

The age of *global* science covers the Cold War and the post-Cold War era of the 20th century onward. In this period, science became a team effort. Laboratories and institutes became the nurseries of new ideas and discoveries.[124]

119　Lewis Pyenson, 'An end to national science: the meaning and the extension of local knowledge,' *History of Science*, vol. 40 (2002), pp. 251-290.

120　Mark Walker, 'The 'national' in international and transnational science,' pp. 359-376.

121　Ibid., p. 376.

122　David Knight, *The Age of Science*, p. 4.

123　Ibid.

124　Ray Spangenburg & Diane Kit Moser, *Modern Science, 1896-1945* (New York, NY: Facts On File, Inc. 2004), p. 172.

While the power of science has often been used to serve the agenda of great power politics, it has also promoted dialogue between nations and helped consolidate international organisations.

These two historical ages for the development of science – the age of science, and the age of global science – align neatly with the actual practice of science diplomacy. First, scientific knowledge was implemented into imperial powers' foreign policy agenda; next, it was used in the foreign policies of the superpowers during the Cold War; and finally, science became a sophisticated and progressive tool in global foreign policy-making. Following the chronology of these periods helps us understand and simplify the ways in which different national styles in science develop.

In brief, a state's intellectual traditions and ways of doing science contribute to the concept of national style in science. One's national style in science plays a role in the emergence and perpetuation of scientific ideas and ideologies and is highly influenced by social institutions and community standards. From the perspective of science diplomacy, what puzzles me is how the universality of science coexists with the pursuit of specific national interests in foreign policy and diplomacy. Put another way, the transparency of science seems to contradict the confidentiality and secrecy of traditional diplomacy by interest-driven nation-states.[125] From this perspective, the crisscrossing patches of science and diplomacy are worth further exploration and have both academic and practical merit.

3.2 *National Style in Diplomacy*

One may say that a state's foreign policy is influenced by pre-existing geographical conditions and regional cultures. A state's geographical location is the starting point from which it sees its place in the world and its manoeuvrability in international relations. This means that its national diplomatic style is more likely to be firmly connected to the geographical and regional attributes in which its culture and traditions were formed than it is to any international standards of diplomacy. However, in the age of global science and globalisation, the universality of diplomatic culture and diplomatic protocols is seen as more attractive than the notion of a national diplomatic style. This does not mean that the universality of diplomatic culture is weakening diplomatic style, but it does make the latter appear less significant.

---

125   Pierre-Bruno Ruffini, *Science and Diplomacy: A New Dimension of International Relations*, p. 37.

In his classical text, prominent British diplomat Harold Nicolson[126] traces the history of diplomacy from its origins and discusses how various diplomatic and national styles impact diplomatic negotiations. Nicolson understands differences in the national diplomatic styles of great powers as caused by variations in national character, traditions, and the requirements of a state's foreign policy.[127] Nicolson argues that foreign policy is shaped by geography and national self-interest that expresses itself in terms of political expediency.[128] A state's national diplomatic style is therefore nothing less than a reflection of its given circumstances and its proposed course of national foreign policy.

The concept of national diplomatic style is meaningful in practice, yet not fully developed in scholarly publications. The most significant (and presumably the only) work strictly devoted to national diplomatic style is by Jeffrey Robertson.[129] Robertson's book was an inspiration for this current study and opened the door towards further examination of the phenomenon of national diplomatic style as a way to understand a state's foreign policy.

The idea to national diplomatic style, Robertson argues, helps to narrow the gap between the scholarly and the practitioner community, at a time when national style is practically acknowledged but not much explored or theorised academically. Robertson proposes a working definition of national diplomatic style: the unique behavioural characteristics used to distinguish the diplomats of one state from another. The concept of national diplomatic style includes both an explicit and tacit acknowledgement of the behavioural characteristics of diplomatic interactions.[130]

I adopt this working definition but add to it one more component: 'improvisation.' Improvisation, a performed sort of resourcefulness, asserts the centrality of embodied practice within a context of limited possibilities.[131] Improvisation might play a crucial role in diplomatic negotiations when diplomats are otherwise struggling to find a resolution or are constrained by protocol.

There one more component that should be acknowledged when defining the behavioural characteristics. Such behavioural varieties represent IR theories in their classical divisions of Realism, Constructivism, and Liberalism.

---

126   Harold Nicolson, *Diplomacy*, (Great Britain: Oxford University Press 1942).
127   Ibid., p. 127.
128   Quoted in: T. G. Otte, 'Nicolson' in G. R. Berridge, Maurice Keens-Soper and T. G. Otte (ed.), *Diplomatic Theory from Machiavelli to Kissinger*, pp. 154-155.
129   Jeffrey Robertson, *Diplomatic Style and Foreign Policy: A Case Study of South Korea* (London and New York: Routledge, 2016).
130   Ibid., p. 53.
131   Jason Dittmer, *Diplomatic Material: Affect, Assemblage, and Foreign Policy*, p. 7.

NATIONAL STYLES IN SCIENCE, DIPLOMACY, AND SCIENCE DIPLOMACY

Brian Rathbun's book[132] explains that diplomacy differs from foreign policy – diplomacy is not the formulation of foreign policy interests but rather the pursuit of them without recourse to the use of force to achieve the same goals. Rathbun shows that the diplomatic style of leaders and diplomats has an important effect on outcomes through the prevailing spirit of negotiations, which is both a function of psychological attributes of individual diplomats as well as party dynamics. Rathburn distinguishes three diplomatic styles – coercive bargaining, pragmatic statecraft, and reasoned dialogue – but attributes styles to an individual's psychological behaviour rather than to national characteristics.

Theorising diplomatic styles through behavioural characteristics, as suggested by Rathbum, is highly relevant to science diplomacy. Diplomatic styles themselves are the product of different psychological motivations which are revealed in decision-makers' ideological predispositions.[133] From this perspective, the adjustment of certain diplomatic styles remains of great value in establishing common ground in diplomatic negotiations and in global governance. The proposed styles match with the main IR and diplomacy theories in which Realism can be asserted as a style of pragmatic statecraft.

There are several other works exploring diplomatic culture in which the notion of style can be detected indirectly. Geoffrey Wiseman, the most prominent academic studying diplomatic culture, addresses the balance between the universalism of diplomatic culture and the particularities of national and regional diplomatic cultures. He suggests that between the universal and national conceptions of diplomatic culture there might be yet another dimension: regional diplomatic culture. Regional diplomatic culture is to be identified by sub-regional variants, or "regional diplomatic complexes."[134] Referring to his earlier paper,[135] Wiseman suggests a modified definition of regional diplomatic culture as one constituted by actors within a self-identified region of three or more sovereign states. By introducing a new concept of regional diplomatic culture, Wiseman proposes further academic exploration in line with

---

132 Brian C. Rathbun, *Diplomacy's Value: Creating Security in 1920s Europe and the Contemporary Middle East*.

133 Ibid., p. 2.

134 Geoffrey Wiseman, 'Evolution of (my) thinking about diplomatic culture,' ISA Annual convention San Francisco 2018, conference paper. Available at http://web.isanet.org/Web/Conferences/San%20Francisco%202018-s/Archive/ce28490c-9dcb-4874-be45-d52c94b49a93.pdf Accessed 7 July, 2018.

135 Geoffrey Wiseman, 'Pax Americana: Bumping into Diplomatic Culture,' *International Studies Perspectives*, vol. 6 (2005), pp. 409-430.

universal (global) and state-based diplomatic culture; he also acknowledges that it is possible to identify national cultures and diplomatic styles.

In an edited volume by Dittmer and McConnell,[136] the relationship between culture and diplomacy is put in focus. This collection of essays follows the notion of diplomacy as a trans-local network of practices through which is seen the vast cultural and political infrastructure that makes state-based diplomacies meaningful. This volume does not directly mention national diplomatic styles, but does acknowledge that national diplomatic cultures both exist and vary geographically.

When international politics is forming at a continental scale (e.g. Europe, Asia, etc.), it often goes through the objects and practices of a national state.[137] Similarly, while analysing scholarly literature on the role of culture in diplomatic negotiations, Trager comes to the conclusion that while cultural context often constrains communication between actors, they can still learn about each other's intentions from formal diplomatic encounters.[138] Even if the goal of diplomacy is not to overcome cultural differences but rather to make negotiations more efficient, it might be said that the notion of the universality in diplomacy indeed exists.[139] That being said, it is still quite an artificial construct represented by diplomatic protocol. For instance, in the context of decolonisation, Opondo says that the diplomatic style adopted by some African countries reflects Edvard Said's concept of Orientalism, an observation that divides diplomatic styles between European and non-European modes.[140] This suggestion might only indicate that universal diplomatic culture or protocol has been adopted by non-European countries as a model of international behaviour during negotiations, while the nature of national style, including diplomatic style, is more likely to remain unchanged.

The notion that there is a universality of diplomacy does not contradict existing differences in national diplomatic style that are derived from national and regional diplomatic practices. The national component in diplomacy is not only an indication of how the national interests of different states can be fulfilled differently by diplomatic work – it is also an indication that national

---

136   Jason Dittmer & Fiona McConnell (ed.), *Diplomatic Cultures and International Politics: Translations, Spaces and Alternatives* (New York, NY: Routledge, 2017).

137   Jason Dittmer, *Diplomatic Material: Affect, Assemblage, and Foreign Policy*, p. 12.

138   Robert F. Trager, *Diplomacy: Communication and the Origins of International Order* (The UK: Cambridge University Press, 2017), pp. 15-16.

139   Ibid., p. 219.

140   Sam Okoth Opondo, 'Decolonising Diplomacy: Reflections on African Estrangement and Exclusion,' in Costas M. Constantinou & James Der Derian (ed.), *Sustainable Diplomacies* (The UK: Palgrave Macmillan 2010), p. 113.

interests may occasionally interfere with the mutual understanding of diplomats. This is because they are the products of not only different national, ethnic and ideological traditions and cultures, but also different diplomatic traditions and cultures.[141] Patterns of culture can be understood as civilisational areas, although there exists an international society which is understood as a society of states.[142] Drawing boundaries between the universal and the national in diplomatic style can be tricky, yet understanding the interdependency between the two is vital for the theory and practice of diplomacy.

3.3 *The Universal and the National*

Just as diplomacy always evolves, so too does national style. Europe has a fascinating historical bonding and continuity of certain diplomatic assets and traditions. The European diplomacy of the Middle Ages started with the rise of resident embassies in Italy in the 15th century and spread throughout Europe in the 16th century, giving bilateral diplomacy its signature institution.[143] The 16th and 17th centuries were predominantly the time for Italian diplomacy, which, in its time, was earlier transmitted to Venice from the Byzantine system.[144] Similarly, ancient Kievan Rus and later Moscovia were highly influenced by, and intentionally adjusted to, the Byzantine style of politics and diplomacy. The flavour of disappearing Byzantine diplomacy was undoubtedly preserved in both West and East Europe. However, the evolving character of diplomatic practices and the change in international politics led to different combinations of the Byzantine legacy: a diplomatic system for West Europe, and political organisation for East Europe emphasising a spiritual and messianic idea for Russia.[145] The civilisational roots inherited from the Byzantine Empire gave rise to European diplomatic patterns long before diplomacy obtained its modern form. That means that the Byzantine style of diplomacy influenced Europe from West and East simultaneously, albeit in different ways.

Since the early 18th century, when Russia emerged as a great power within the European system,[146] the commonality of diplomatic culture and protocol

---

141 Tatiana V. Zonova, 'Diplomatic Cultures: Comparing Russia and the West in Terms of a 'Modern Model of Diplomacy,' *The Hague Journal of Diplomacy*, vol. 2 (2007), pp. 1-23.

142 Christian Reus-Smit, 'Cultural Diversity and International Order,' *International Organisation* vol. 71 (2017), pp. 851-885.

143 Geoffrey Wiseman, 'Pax Americana: Bumping into Diplomatic culture,' *International Studies Perspectives* vol. 6, (2005), p. 411.

144 Harold Nicolson, *Diplomacy*, p. 43.

145 Tatiana Zonova, 'Diplomatic Cultures: Comparing Russia and the West in Terms of a 'Modern Model of Diplomacy," pp. 1-23.

146 Loren R. Graham, 'Big Science in the Last Years of the Big Soviet Union,' *Osiris*, 7 (1992), pp. 49-71.

prevailed, even as national and cultural characteristics remained distinct. The phenomenon of commonality in modern diplomacy traces back to the Treaties of Westphalia, when the modern state and the diplomatic and military disposition of Europe began to take shape. War was intended to reinforce the balance of power, while diplomacy became an instrument in which the negotiations in Westphalia served as a model.[147] The 'Westphalian' state – also known as the utopian state – is the only form of governance that has been truly universalised since the late 18th century. Despite its longevity, the future of the Westphalian state is not certain: it might yet decline in power in the 21st century[148] due to challenges from non-Western emerging powers, whether it is the reassertion of Islamic values or an increasingly confident China developing its own international paradigms and promoting its own traditional values.[149]

China, as the only Asian entity among the P5 Countries, is unique for its history, culture, political values, and policies. Despite its differences with the West, China nevertheless adapted universal norms of diplomacy and science that allowed the country to gain economic power and start playing an important role in international politics, and to use mechanisms and tools in dealings with Western powers.

The universal and the national – whether in science or diplomacy – are contrasting but merged categories. While it is relatively easy to distinguish each category in its own right, it is undoubtedly harder to define the borders between the national and the universal and to measure their mutual interdependence. Diving into the distinct national components of each country's diplomacy, through illuminating a series of elements characterising national style in science and diplomacy, could help us comprehend science diplomacy and identify ways to implement it for global governance.

3.4 *National Style in Science Diplomacy and Global Governance*

In this section I suggest a way to add another element to science diplomacy's well-known taxonomy. Three dimensions of science diplomacy are commonly cited by scholars: (1) science in diplomacy; (2) diplomacy for science; and (3) science for diplomacy. To this list I suggest adding: (4) science diplomacy for global governance. Evaluating great powers' national styles in science diplomacy is essential, as it indicates the potential for collaborative global governance of the kind that could improve the world on a massive systematic

---

147   Jason Dittmer. *Diplomatic Material: Affect, Assemblage, and Foreign Policy*, p. 12.

148   Jo Guldi & David Armitage, *The History Manifesto*, p. 76.

149   Anthony Milner, 'Culture and the international relations of Asia,' *The Pacific Review*, vol. 30, no. 6 (2017), pp. 857-869.

NATIONAL STYLES IN SCIENCE, DIPLOMACY, AND SCIENCE DIPLOMACY

scale. Seeing certain patterns in power accumulation, evaluating great powers' international behaviour, and highlighting constructive elements of national styles in science diplomacy, are pragmatic and rational steps forward for international policy-making.

The world is now witnessing the difficult birth of a multipolar system – one that will challenge the existing world order dominated by the West. This new rapidly evolving situation requires reconsidering and reimagining the circumstances in which science progresses and in which scientific advantages are used to shape the international system. The economic rise of non-Western powers with a focus on technology, and the emergence of non-Western diplomacies, constitute a new situation. Non-Western players are seeking opportunities to build their own international influence during this period of power transition. The Western diplomatic system, the Westphalian system, and society of states are no longer as exclusionary as they used to be.[150] If the science diplomacy push towards global governance has any force, then academics and practitioners must understand countries' differing national styles in science diplomacy. This understanding can be both a way to secure a substantial place for Western powers in the emerging multipolar world, and a set of instructions for others in preserving global political stability.

Historically, the pursuit of regional or international influence has been based on the accumulation and practical use of scientific knowledge. A state's scientific and technological advancements were also a bargaining chip when great powers interacted, competed, and cooperated with one another. As a result of such interactions, Europe and the West forged ahead of the rest of the world,[151] leading to a great global divergence in wealth and power. Victorian England became a model for civil agreement, relative equality, participatory democracy, and declared opportunities for all.[152] The imperialism of the late 19th century and the great divergence forced the rest of the world to adjust to Western dominance and adopt Western diplomacy. Now, in the 21st century, diplomacy has become a polite form of neo-colonialism whereby the West has co-opted the newly independent states of Africa and Asia.[153] Diplomacy has gotten a reputation as a universal tool in maintaining state-state relations.

---

150 Costas M. Constantinou & James Der Derian, "Sustaining Global Hope: Sovereignty, Power and the Transformation of Diplomacy,' in Costas M. Constantinou and James Der Derian (ed.), *Sustainable Diplomacies* (The UK: Palgrave Macmillan 2010), p. 12.

151 Philip T. Hoffman, 'Why Was It Europeans Who Conquered the World?' *The Journal of Economic History*, vol. 72, no. 3 (September 2012), pp. 601-633.

152 Jo Guldi & David Armitage, *The History Manifesto*, p. 57.

153 Stuart Murray, et. al. 'The Present and Future of Diplomacy and Diplomatic Studies,' *International Studies Review*, vol. 13 (2011), pp. 709-728.

Assuming that in pursuing their national interests, states act in line with Realism, then acquiring more power and maintaining the balance of force is something that characterises the contemporary world order. Although the scope of disputes between great powers and smaller powers might be expanding, a sudden change towards cooperation between adversaries remains possible. The underlying objectives of science diplomacy indicate that states have an awareness of global challenges and can show willingness to address security dilemmas and break dangerous deadlocks. Science diplomacy is a way to put a finger on the planet's pulse and assess the potential for the world not only to maintain the peace but also take steps towards global governance.

The idea of global governance fits well with the ambitious scope and abilities of great powers' assertive behaviour, as it is explained by the framework of Realism. Understanding the nature of great power behaviour and identifying national styles in science diplomacy might eventually smooth the transition towards global governance, should there be such an opportunity. The issues in need of collaborative governance are already on the agenda in international policy-making. When a role for scientific institutions is clearly defined, is supported by national governments, and is given national diplomatic assistance, building international coalitions will let science diplomacy be the main way for states to adhere to the goals of global governance. Engaging in science diplomacy is a question of making a rational choice: to enable the world to balance on the scales of international harmonious integration. Science diplomacy for global governance might therefore be the most important task to be performed by the great powers.

Part 2

The constructive elements of national style in science and diplomacy are based on a pre-existing system of forces and historical path dependencies and can be fruitfully discussed. Part 2 of this study turns to empirical cases of the United Nations Security Council's five permanent members. Because each country has its own specific historical and cultural characteristics, national styles in science and diplomacy are sometimes viewed and represented unevenly. Much like national style in science *and* diplomacy, national style in science diplomacy can be shown through its constructive elements. Each empirical case is a way to test the hypotheses of state behaviour, thereby making progress in implementing science diplomacy in foreign policy-making and analysing a state's potential to use science diplomacy for global governance. The soft power of science diplomacy has been assessed to be a power of influence for the global good. By contrast, while the idea of national style in science, diplomacy, and science diplomacy, might be viewed quite idealistically, the reality is more complex and continuously evolving.

4 United Kingdom

4.1 *Scientific Pragmatism and Ethics*

With the beginning of the age of science, British modern science developed foundational scientific disciplines to align with the programs of the British Association for the Advancement of Science.[154] The Association set boundaries that, in the English-speaking world, separated 'science' from the arts, humanities and (later) the social sciences. This disciplinary division turned out to be more stable than most political boundaries.[155] I refrain myself from listing all scientific achievements and historical periods in which science in Britain has been developed, as all these issues are extensively discussed in the disciplines of history and philosophy of science. I instead attempt to distinguish elements that link Britain's national style in science to modern science diplomacy practices, in order to understand these practices and recognise how states behave when they are developing a toolbox of science diplomacy.

Britain's national style in science and scientific way of thinking are viewed as a dichotomy between the autonomy of the sciences on the one hand, and religious dogmatism on the other. The country's interest in natural sciences reflected intellectual concerns about understanding how the world was 'designed,' how the universe works, and what man's place in it is. The observation that an organism functions as a unity was taken as proof that God had designed it.[156] In this sense, the mixed desire to obtain knowledge about the world led Britain to value knowledge for its practical uses. The pragmatism and practicality of British science was expanded by the possibilities provided by its empire. For instance, fields like geology or biology that needed a global laboratory[157] have been well advanced because the British Empire had such a 'global laboratory.'

Religion in Britain was no great obstacle to the country obtaining knowledge of the natural sciences; at the same time there was also very little anti-clericalism. This dynamic was well managed and perfectly fit into the country's system of Victorian values as the pressure to believe in God developed into a

---

154 David Knight, *The Age of Science*, p. 8.
155 Ibid., p. 4.
156 Ibid., p. 55.
157 John Gascoigne, 'Science and the British Empire from its Beginnings to 1850' in Brett M. Bennett & Joseph M. Hodge (ed.), *Science and Empire. Knowledge and Networks of Science across the British Empire, 1800-1970* (The UK: Palgrave Macmillan 2011), p. 63.

religion-driven morality. Nor was religiosity an obstacle in building the British Empire; the empire needed to be sustained by belief. Such beliefs justified the position of the conquerors and their imperial might. One of the most common arguments of the imperialists was the belief that their rule brought with it greater prosperity based on the rational ordering of nature.[158] Britain's pragmatic strategy for the advancement of knowledge within its empire required a commitment on the part of the British state. This commitment was slow to be realised, in part due to the mentality of British elites during the formative period of the empire. Thus, pragmatism, practicality, and ethical considerations can be distinguished as essential elements of Britain's style in science.

Another aspect of British national style in science is scientism (scientific spirit) and education. As an advanced maritime power, Britain led scientific voyages and built an empire in which men of science were often in charge. Proper education, devotion to facts, and practical knowledge became fundamental attributes. Science was a form of public knowledge that made sense of practical life questions, rather than a secret craft or religious mystery. A growing reputation for science led to more progress and imperial expansion.[159] The country's scientific voyages and imperial expansion of the 19th century helped spread scientism throughout Western Europe, the US, Russia and Japan,[160] as new emerging powers needed ways to either adopt or catch up with Britain's scientific progress. The scientism of the 20th century represented new standards for understanding science, as the academic study of science became institutionalised as an intellectual revolution and historical craft.[161]

The *age of global science* not only made science a global asset, but also led people to recognise the complexity of scientific integration and the need for international collaboration and further developments in foreign affairs.[162] The real value of British science lies in its credibility and overall reception. The involvement of the British scientific community – their institutions, academies, laboratories, and universities – into efforts for international collaboration affected British foreign policy in two progressive ways. First, the transparency, credibility, and effectiveness of British science made it a dominant force in intellectual and practical life. These characteristics make the country's science,

---

158   Ibid., p. 48.
159   Ibid., p. 51.
160   David Knight, *The Age of Science*, p. 148.
161   Anna-K. Mayer, 'Setting up a discipline, II: British history of science and "the end of ideology," 1931-1948,' *Studies in History and Philosophy of Science*, vol. 35 (2004), pp. 41-72.
162   David C. Clary, 'A Scientist in the Foreign Office,' *Science & Diplomacy* (September 2013). Available at: http://www.sciencediplomacy.org/editorial/2013/scientist-in-foreign-office. Accessed 8 August, 2018.

NATIONAL STYLES IN SCIENCE, DIPLOMACY, AND SCIENCE DIPLOMACY   43

as well as the country, attractive and influential. Second, Britain's scientific community acknowledges that scientific progress brings with it an ethical responsibility for things such as human well-being and climate change. For instance, questions of scientific and social responsibility, war, and morality, have all become a part of the culture of Britain's nuclear scientists.[163] These assets of Britain's national style in science tend directly towards science diplomacy as an effective diplomatic toolbox – one that advances this major power in promoting its foreign policy agenda.

4.2   *Diplomacy of Realism and Diplomacy of Possibility*

In line with the Realist tradition of great power diplomacy, Britain's diplomacy itself is an element of power. 'Old diplomacy', as it has been traditionally called, is premised upon a policy of maintaining a balance of power in regions vital to British interests, and using the military and financial resources of the state to underpin this policy.[164] Britain is often cited as an example of a country that can be equally strong in multiple elements of power, such as military strength, wealth and population.[165]

Since the foundation of the British Foreign Office in 1782, Britain has become a leader in the evolution of modern diplomacy and foreign policy formation.[166] The Foreign Office has a reputation as a knowledge-based organisation with efficient information management procedures geared towards informed policy-making and overseeing the country's diplomatic strategy.[167] Britain's diplomatic strategy aims, predictably, to secure British geopolitical interests, with professional diplomats providing the strategic basis of British foreign policy.

In its early days, the country's diplomatic corps had the character of an aristocracy with little bureaucracy, and represented separated diplomatic services appended to the government's domestic responsibilities. The diplomatic service was primarily responsible for the representation of consular services abroad. Over the course of the Victorian Era and the global change

---

163   Thaddeus Trenn, 'The central role of energy in Soddy's holistic and critical approach to nuclear science, economics, and social responsibility,' *BJHS*, vol. 12 (1979), pp. 261-276; Jonathan Hogg & Christoph Laucht, 'Introduction: British nuclear culture,' *BJHS*, vol. 45, no. 4 (December 2012), pp. 479-493.

164   B. J. C. McKercher, 'The Foreign Office, 1930-39: Strategy, Permanent Interests and National Security,' *Contemporary British History*, vol. 18, no. 3 (2004), p. 87.

165   Paul Sharp, *Diplomatic Theory of International Relations*, p. 56.

166   Jason Dittmer, *Diplomatic Material: Affect, Assemblage, and Foreign Policy*, p. 25.

167   T. G. Otte, 'Old Diplomacy: Reflections on the Foreign Office before 1914,' *Contemporary British History*, vol. 18, no. 3, (2004), p. 31.

of the 20th century, the diplomatic service became more strictly attached to the Foreign Office. The latter for its part, became one of the most powerful ministries to formulate foreign policy and establish and maintain diplomatic negotiations with new states and territories.

This new situation affected the organisational structure of the Foreign Office significantly, making it an epicentre of the state's policymaking.[168] It produced practical policies able to protect British interests and selected only men from certain social backgrounds to implement such policies. The relative homogeneity of the class and educational background of professional diplomats meant that academic qualifications, especially a good honours degree, were essential for entering the diplomatic profession and being placed in important embassies overseas.[169] Serving for the Foreign Office was perceived as one of the most socially exclusive and prestigious occupations.[170]

Professional British diplomats understood the reality of power, and for the most part produced effective diplomatic strategy. Such strategy merely reflected the goal of Realism to see the world as it is, not as it should be, while maintaining a balance of power with other states that shared Britain's interests.[171] Here, the phenomenon of the Anglosphere enhanced British hegemony throughout the Victorian Era. Britain's diplomatic strategy may be taken as a prototype of the founding traditions and theories of Realism in international relations and diplomacy, especially those coming from the English IR school. The 'old diplomacy' of Realism is therefore a key element of Britain's diplomatic style.

Another structural element of British diplomatic style – assemblages of circulating materialities that compose the Foreign Office – directly relates to scientific and technological progress since the age of science. New technological innovations of the time were effectively adopted by the Foreign Office, enabling it to expand its reach and correspond with any embassy around the globe. The invention of the telegraph, the growing sophistication of printing technologies, and a supply cheap paper greatly aided the growth of British diplomacy. The exponential rise of the assemblages of papers and other materials also led to the emergence of bureaucracy.

In this context, bureaucracy should not necessarily be taken in its usual negative connotation as an obstacle to policy implementation. With a number of reforms and reorganisations, the Foreign Office made its bureaucracy highly

---

168   Jason Dittmer, *Diplomatic Material: Affect, Assemblage, and Foreign Policy*, p. 26.

169   T. G. Otte, 'Old Diplomacy: Reflections on the Foreign Office before 1914,' p. 34.

170   B. J. C. McKercher, 'The Foreign Office, 1930-39: Strategy, Permanent Interests and National Security,' p. 90.

171   Ibid., p. 104.

professional in efficient information management procedures, informed policy-making, and decisive action.[172] Competence in work with assemblages of papers made British diplomacy more procedural and effective. As a result, the UK took a historically leading role in forging geopolitical assemblages.[173] This element of Britain's national style of diplomacy – the professional forging of geopolitical assemblages – has been exceptionally valuable in the emergence of alliances and other long-standing institutional arrangements, such as multinational international organisations formed in response to the conditions of globalisation.

Maintaining a finely balanced European continental equilibrium, while at the same time protecting national interests globally, are perceived to be the main assets of British foreign policy. In this sense, British diplomacy has remained very much consistent since the 19th century in its showcasing of a 'diplomacy of possibility.' I do not consider 'diplomacy of possibility' as another element of national diplomatic style; rather, I see it as a branch of the 'diplomacy of Realism' that primarily aims to maintain the balance of power and grow influence.

Despite all the trouble it has evidently created for British foreign policy, the Brexit phenomenon can be taken as an example of 'diplomacy of possibility.' From a diplomatic view, it might be that Brexit itself is a manifestation of the diplomacy of Realism, with the aim to maintain a balance of power in Europe and hold the national interests of Britain above the interests of the European Union. The Foreign Office's 'old diplomacy,' the Anglosphere, the professionalism of diplomats, the wide network of embassies and high commissions abroad, and the ability to forge geopolitical assemblages – all of these things demonstrate Britain's 'diplomacy of possibility'.

It might also be that Brexit is a sign not of a crisis of liberalism but rather a turn towards a realist balance of power. The decision to leave could be seen as a means to protect the liberal order of the British Isles from diverse European nations and political systems. Brexit could also be an attempt to reinforce British influence by expanding the Anglosphere and enhancing relations with the English-speaking world as it was at the height of British hegemony in the Victorian Era.

A final element of Britain's style in diplomacy is its aesthetic component. Jason Dittmer suggests that this is the "more-than-human nature of diplomatic practices and the affective forces that shape the spaces in which policymaking

---

172   T. G. Otte, 'Old Diplomacy: Reflections on the Foreign Office before 1914,' p. 36.

173   Jason Dittmer, *Diplomatic Material: Affect, Assemblage, and Foreign Policy*, p. 19.

occurs."[174] By 'more-than-human nature', Dittmer refers to the process of producing and circulating diplomatic materials, which is central in everyday diplomatic practices. The physical space of the Foreign Office building and its architecture might underline the specifics of British diplomacy with its concern for a visually effective atmosphere for efficient government. Jeffrey Robertson agrees with this idea and argues that British diplomatic architecture, whether of embassies and consulates or foreign ministries, is the symbolic representation of the power, prestige, influence, and culture of a country.[175] The aesthetic component impacts national diplomatic style by becoming a part of it.

Britain's diplomatic strategy permitted the maintenance of the balance of power in the world which is so vital to British security. The efficiency of British diplomacy lies in both its innovation and its consistency with 'old diplomacy' – the former can be seen in the country's willingness to develop and deploy new ways of conducting diplomacy. One of the most efficient and long-term types of diplomacy, and one most oriented towards the long term, is science diplomacy. It is a diplomacy for which the UK is a world leader.

4.3   *A Trendsetter in Science Diplomacy*

The UK's vision, understanding, and implementation of science diplomacy are exceptional. The interdependency between the use of scientific knowledge in foreign policy and continuous scientific development was one of the main reasons why Britain was able to sustain its hegemony during the Victorian Era. Likewise, I suggest that its science diplomacy of the 21st century is one of the instruments best able to sustain Britain's position as a great power. British science diplomacy is also an approach that fits well with a Realist approach to foreign policy.

The official history of British science diplomacy started as late as 2009, with government's announcement that it would create a new role of Chief Scientific Adviser to the Foreign Office, bringing science to the frontline of international policymaking and diplomacy.[176] Britain's former Chief Scientific Advisers to the Foreign Office, David C. Clary and his successor Robin W. Grimes, have done a tremendous job in establishing science as a tool in Britain's diplomatic toolbox. They promoted the use of scientific evidence and science networks to place science collaboration at the heart of Britain's key international relationships. When analysing Britain's science diplomacy, I distinguish three

---

174   Ibid., p. 27.

175   Jeffrey Robertson, *Diplomatic Style and Foreign Policy: A Case Study of South Korea*, pp. 27-28.

176   David C. Clary, 'A Scientist in the Foreign Office.'

categories of countries with which Britain aims to cooperate: developed countries, (re)emerging scientific powers, and the recipience countries of official development assistance (ODA).

Before elaborating on each category, I note that the effectiveness of British science diplomacy relies upon its advancement of the sciences, wide network of embassies and consulates abroad, and involvement of non-state actors. In 2017, the Lowy Institute's Global Diplomacy Index ranked the UK seventh in the world, with a network of 225 total diplomatic posts.[177] These diplomatic posts represent the country in its various relations, including continuous support for world-class science and innovation collaboration. Embassies and consulates themselves are the tools that strengthen interstate relations. As far as non-state actors go, the British Council and the Royal Society take the lead in disseminating Britain's wide range of scientific activities. They use the network of British embassies to organise and promote educational programs, scientific conferences, seminars, workshops, and lectures, while also putting in foreign and British scientists in contact with one another.

When it comes to developed countries, Britain aims to sustain and strengthen interstate relations, while continuously maintaining ongoing multinational and multilateral scientific projects that require diplomatic assistance. This kind of collaboration includes the proceedings of international treaties as the Antarctic Treaty and the Non-Proliferation Treaty, partaking in multinational scientific projects such as CERN, the Arctic Council, the International Space Station, or the Intergovernmental Panel on Climate Change. Britain's activities with developed countries fit in the *diplomacy for science* dimension of science diplomacy.

With (re)emerging scientific powers such as Russia and Brazil, Britain aims to gain influence over and intensify mutually beneficial bilateral scientific cooperation. The 2017 UK-Russia Year of Science and Education, which I have already discussed, is the primary example for this category. Britain's main scientific collaborative project with Russian scientists is anti-microbial resistance; with Brazilian scientists it is joining forces on Alzheimer research. This second category of countries might constitute the *science for diplomacy* dimension. Here, Britain aims to improve damaged relations with Russia and foster interstate relations with Brazil.

If the objectives pursued by British science diplomacy in dealings with scientifically advanced and (re)emerging scientific powers are mostly pragmatic, then Britain's engagement with the third category of countries – recipients of ODA – has different objectives. With these countries, Britain is pursuing

---

177 More on the website: http://globaldiplomacyindex.lowyinstitute.org.

economic and research investments. The priorities of Britain's science diplomacy with the ODA-recipient countries revolve around their economic development challenges. To explain Britain's diplomatic progress with ODA recipients, it is helpful to look at it through the perspective of the Foreign Office's Newton Fund, launched in 2014.[178] The Newton Fund, a series of investments in research, aims to develop partnerships in science, innovation, economic development, and welfare, and to promote British interests globally.

Hugo Swire, Britain's former Foreign Office Minister for Science, formulated several science diplomacy initiatives to promote British foreign policy. First, he allowed Britain's network of embassies overseas to be used by British scientists looking to build international partnerships. Second, this network can then mobilise and coordinate international scientific action on specific cross-border issues that are of strategic significance to the UK. Third, Britain's scientific prowess is a huge part of the British brand be promoted worldwide.[179]

The objectives of Britain's Newton Fund and resulting scientific cooperation might sound somewhat optimistic, considering the level of economic and scientific development of ODA recipients. In this sense, the announced objectives hold a great promise shared responsibility for the future as a way to elevate human well-being and build productive long-term international relations. This means that the partnerships with ODA countries are supposed to foster mutual respect and commitment. The promotion of bilateral and multilateral science collaboration is intended to benefit the diplomatic process through building trust and understandings at a personal level via people-to-people exchanges. Science diplomacy objectives are the means to secure the foundations for long-term relations based on common goals and shared responsibility for global issues.[180]

Science diplomacy with ODA recipients is a long-term strategy in building influence and demonstrating the attractiveness of the UK through its soft power. It is not merely for the promotion of British science or the spread of British power, and it is also not purely a gesture of goodwill, even though these objectives can be reasonably applied. Instead, scientific activities with ODA-recipient countries are concrete steps to demonstrate Britain's scientific and

---

178   More on the website: http://www.newtonfund.ac.uk.

179   Hugo Swire, 'The UK, Brazil and Science Diplomacy,' a speech delivered on 15 December 2014. Available at: https://www.gov.uk/government/speeches/the-uk-brazil-and-science-diplomacy. Accessed 9 August, 2018.

180   Robin W. Grimes & Claire McNulty, 'The Newton Fund: Science and Innovation for Development and Diplomacy,' *Science & Diplomacy* (December 2016). Available at: http://www.sciencediplomacy.org/article/2016/newton-fund-science-and-innovation-for-development-and-diplomacy. Accessed 8 August, 2018.

moral authority, as well as its ethical responsibility as a wealthy and advanced power. Funding scientific and educational projects gives Britain the potential to build and sustain good relations with the ODA recipients. This strategy will help these countries build their own well-being, reduce the risk of conflict, and prospectively join forces to resolve global issues.

To summarise, under the umbrella of science diplomacy, the UK embraces various joint scientific projects ranging from work on global issues to advancing the local well-being of ODA countries. Britain's national style in science diplomacy can be recognised within those activities that serve diplomatic goals by promoting science abroad. Some activities are underpinned by a shared vision on the openness, transparency, integrity and universality of the sciences, regardless of cultural differences, religions, or languages. Considering the consequences of Britain's status as a great power in colonial and post-colonial times, science diplomacy might eventually become the main instrument of British soft power. The soft power of science diplomacy is generated not only through scientific and educational attractiveness and research opportunities, but also through (re)building trust and making commitments with other countries.

A Realist approach in promoting its national interests, restoring relations when needed, and gaining influence with emerging scientific powers and underdeveloped countries, is the main feature of Britain's national style of science diplomacy. In sum, Britain's scientific development, its capacity in providing professional expertise and ethical guidance, its wide diplomatic network, and its leadership in managing global assemblages, are strong arguments for British foreign policy to consider science diplomacy as a toolbox for global governance in the shaping of world politics.

5   France

5.1   *The Inseparability of the French State and Science*
Ideas of liberty that go back to the French Revolution and French colonial empire impacted the formation of the country's style in science. The fall of Bastille saw the dawn of scientific development in France and the general adoption of materialism and unitarianism. The history of French science is the story of statecraft and interactions between the state and science, which has been one of partnership rather than of partisanship.[181] This partnership

---

181   Mary Jo Nye, 'Recent Sources and Problems in the History of French Science,' *Historical Studies in the Physical Sciences*, vol. 13, no. 2 (1983), p. 404.

was more associated with serving the state out of civic virtue than personal advantage, and eventually made science a career comparable to any other state career.

The inseparability of science and the French state could be dangerous in times of political crisis. Scientists became powerless when the state's power was questioned or rejected. Distrust of scientists as state experts frequently surfaced when the regime changed. For example, Antoine Lavoisier, the prominent French chemist, was guillotined during the French Revolution. The element of inseparability of science and the state evolved into a safer construct with the emergence of scientific expertise that, in its time, fostered development of science as a professional career.

A scientist's possession of knowledge became an asset of the French state in the building of the technocratic elite. At the end the late 19th century, the technocratic elite consisted of students, including those recruited from the lower bourgeoisie. Recruitment and career advancement went with merit-based selection and numerous exams, establishing the notion of science as a career and the scientific profession as a means of social mobility.

The view of science as a profession led to a situation in which career scientists, also known as 'generalists,' were equipped by encyclopaedic knowledge and methodological training but lacked practical knowledge and skills.[182] While the natural sciences were a better fit for the British predisposition for discovering 'God's laws,' there are distinct disciplines in which France has its own comparative advantage – chemistry, astronomy, and mathematics, in which a methodological approach to science prevailed. However, France's traditions of public debate and scientific expertise then distinguished a significant group of practical scientists, namely 'specialists', who were formally separated from the group of 'generalists.' Another division within the French style in science was the divide between common general scientific culture and narrow specialised activity – put simply, French sciences were labelled as either theoretical or applied. However, Mary Jo Nye, a prominent historian of science, argues that such distinction was not actually as strict as we might see it today, but rather reflected France's different educational tracks for social and administrative purposes. Regardless, scientific progress proceeded despite the formal labels.[183]

During the *age of science*, France lost its national rivalry with Britain, as it was unable to turn scientific knowledge into state power to the extent Britain was able to.[184] France suffered a decline in scientific progress during the two

---

182   Ibid., p. 408.
183   Ibid., p. 411.
184   David Knight, *The Age of Science*, p. 17.

NATIONAL STYLES IN SCIENCE, DIPLOMACY, AND SCIENCE DIPLOMACY 51

World Wars, and had to put much effort into reconstruction in the post-war period. The Cold War turned global attention toward the Soviet-American rivalry, making France focus on shrinking its technological gap in military and nuclear fields. Awareness of the importance of science and technology at official levels was acute enough. The Fifth Republic has renewed the relationship between science and state. Now the partnership between the two has emerged as an official *French science policy* which is dated from the beginning of the Charles de Gaulle presidency in 1959. The relations between 'generalists' and 'specialists' and between research institutions and industry have been a part of this policy. De Gaulle saw research and innovation as key to securing France a place on the world stage, and helped to create France's world-leading nuclear and space research and build defence and transport industries. The improvement of the state-led liaison with science,[185] alongside the process of nationalising industrial companies,[186] is one of the evolved characteristics of the inseparability of the French state and science. The initiation of *French science policy* occurred during the watershed moment between the *age of science* and the *age of global science.*

With the inseparability of French state and science and the notion of science as a career as a starting point, we can see both the legacy of the development of science in France and the challenges it faces. One particular challenge is France's hierarchical system of science organisations and research communities. French research has long been dominated by a 'mandarinate' – a hierarchy that concentrates funds and vests power in a relatively small number of laboratories and institutes.[187] The 'mandarinate' rules most science and technology incubators as they have received the majority of government science funding. This system makes French science dependent on the country's economic situation (and therefore foreign policy), and is vulnerable if funding decreases. On the other hand, if the scientific hierarchy is effective at producing knowledge, that can boost the economy and give French science even more funding.[188]

State guardianship and the dominance of the 'mandarinate' might look like a flexible system for those scientists and laboratories devoted only to conducting research and doing good science, as it relieves them of the stress of competition and ensuring their research is commercially viable. As a result, this system allowed France to conduct world-class research and maintain a

---

185   John Walsh, 'Some New Targets Defined for French Science Policy,' p. 626.

186   Pierre-Bruno Ruffini, *Science and Diplomacy: A New Dimension of International Relations,* p. 97.

187   Michael Balter, 'Storming the Bastille,' *Science,* vol. 296 (26 April 2002), p. 649.

188   John Walsh, 'Some New Targets Defined for French Science Policy,' *Science,* vol. 156 (5 May 1967), p. 630.

position as a scientifically advanced country, making great strides in defence, nuclear research, aerospace and health research. However, France's embrace of the bureaucracy and hierarchy put French science in a competitive disadvantage with the science of America. This has led to the so-called 'brain drain' of French scientists leaving France for the US,[189] and makes the country's science agenda the subject of continuous state-initiated reforms.

French science policy might, to some extent, be considered a part of science diplomacy, but I see it mostly as the evolution and continuity of the inseparability phenomena. *French science policy* itself became an instrument of reform in the country's system of science during recent decades, frequently directing scientists to return the Gaullist movement to its true research roots. France's science policy not only aims to make the country's science go global and foster international cooperation, but also to make these scientific aspirations a critical part of French statecraft and long-term diplomatic strategy.

5.2   *'Movement' Diplomacy and Diplomacy of 'Cohabitation'*
Like the British, French diplomacy is the implementation of its foreign policy strategy. It is traditionally represented in consular diplomacy as serving national residents abroad and maintaining interests of commercial intermediation. During the period of colonial maritime discoveries and imperialism, French diplomacy was marked by running of consulates and cultural networks in order to enhance French influence on local elites – for instance, in francophone Africa.

One of the main elements of French diplomatic style in the *age of science* was the strong relationship between political and cultural activities. The sciences, the arts, and literature were prerequisites to diplomatic relations and facilitated diplomatic negotiations.[190] Reflecting the cultural component of French diplomacy, up until the end of World War One, France's diplomatic corps was primarily aristocratic. Aristocracy was the carrier of one's educational and cultural background and was a tradition of public service, including the highest positions within the Department of Foreign Affairs.

Similar to career scientists, the professionalisation of French career diplomats was imposed on social and intellectual criteria. Competitive exams for career diplomats were run in France from 1880. Diplomats were supposed to observe rules of a specific sociability that placed great importance on ceremony and rites of protocol. Social relations, as well as belonging to transnational,

---

189   Alexei V. Shestopal & Nikolay V. Litvak, 'Science Diplomacy: French Experience,' p. 110.
190   Philippe Lane, *French Scientific and Cultural Diplomacy* (The UK: Liverpool University Press, 2013), p. 8.

NATIONAL STYLES IN SCIENCE, DIPLOMACY, AND SCIENCE DIPLOMACY 53

familial, academic, and cultural networks, were bound to have influence in the conducting of business, persuasion, and the circulation of information.[191] The aristocracy genuinely relied on their relations and connections, and spread France's social model and cultural practices over national diplomatic elites while bringing them into the circles of political power.[192]

The social composition of French diplomatic corps started to change in the *age of global science*, making a steady transition away from an aristocracy rooted in bourgeoisie-based recruitment, even if it was not yet so accessible to the working class. If the main task of French diplomats of the 19th century was to keep the balance of power in the context of the Concert of Europe, then after the World Wars the goal of diplomats was to contribute to the development of new nations, thereby aiding collective security and the process of European integration.[193]

The Cold War and post-Cold War eras added new elements to French foreign policy and diplomacy. France continued to promote its influence through the expansion of cultural networks, educational programs and technical cooperation but also included a number of export industries such as agriculture, aviation, defence and nuclear technology. The Department of Foreign Affairs concentrated on initiatives to benefit education, health, archaeology and technology.[194] Even the French language itself became the source of defending and promoting France's role in international organisations.

Such activities can be looked at through the lens of the geopolitical rivalries which limited French international influence. In this context, one element of French diplomacy that has been adopted is the notion of 'movement diplomacy' – a diplomacy of bold initiatives and strong moves.[195] French 'movement diplomacy' has been used as an instrument to compensate the limits of French international influence that was strained by historical competition, first with Great Britain, then with the US and the Soviet Union, and now by the US and, perhaps, China.

---

191 Isabelle Dasque, 'Diplomats and Diplomacy, *Encyclopédie pour une histoire nouvelle de l'Europe*, (9 November, 2017). Available at https://ehne.fr/en/article/political -epistemology/elites-privileged-vehicles-construction-europe/diplomats-and-diplomacy. Accessed 6 August, 2018.

192 Isabelle Dasque, 'La diplomatie française au lendemain de la Grande Guerre. Bastion d'une aristocratie au service de l'État?' *Vingtième Siècle. Revue d'histoire*, 2008/3 (n° 99), p. 33.

193 Isabelle Dasque, 'Diplomats and Diplomacy.'

194 Philippe Lane, *French Scientific and Cultural Diplomacy*, pp. 11-12.

195 Richard Balme, 'Revisiting French diplomacy in the age of globalisation,' *French Politics*, vol. 8, no. 1, (2010), p. 92.

The spectrum of contemporary 'movement diplomacy' mechanisms extends from conceiving of finance as an instrument of diplomacy[196] to forming secret alliances and providing technological assistance. Below, I include examples of movement diplomacy as they relate to science diplomacy, at least insofar as they include the two essential components, science and diplomacy. The first example is the secret French-American collaboration for uranium in Morocco in the 1950s – a partnership also known as uranium diplomacy.[197] A second example is the "Forum of Four" – the failed French initiative of 1969 to bring about diplomatic cooperation between the United States, the Soviet Union, Britain, and France, to put to an end the Arab-Israeli conflict.[198] A final example is ongoing French and Pakistani negotiations for nuclear development in the second half for the 20th century.[199] Considering the questionable outcomes of these diplomatic initiatives, it seems to me more reasonable to characterise these examples more as 'movement diplomacy' than science diplomacy.

'Movement diplomacy' goes hand-in-hand with 'cohabitation diplomacy', a diplomacy that seeks agreements (also known as 'territorial diplomacy'). Cohabitation diplomacy is another element marking France's national diplomatic style. For example, in the 'crowded' Europe of the 19th century, it is estimated that major European powers were at war approximately 30 per cent of the time.[200] The atrocity of the two World Wars also had an enormous impact on European nations, leading them to consolidate and find ways to maintain a continuous peace.

Interestingly, volumes of French diplomatic documents published by the French Ministry of Foreign Affairs in 1954 were concerned with the prelude to wars, including the years leading up to 1870, 1914, and 1939. The intention was to show France's innocence in the outbreak of these conflicts.[201] While not rejecting its past responsibility, but rather to show its post-war intentions, French diplomacy has outlined its future priorities towards European

---

196 John Keiger, 'Wielding Finance as a Weapon of Diplomacy: France and Britain in the 1920s,' *Contemporary British History*, vol. 25, no. 1, (2011), pp. 29-47.

197 Matthew Adamson, 'Les liaisons dangereuses: resource surveillance, uranium diplomacy and secret French–American collaboration in 1950s Morocco,' *BJHS*, vol. 49, no. 1 (March 2016), pp. 79-105.

198 Yehuda U. Blanga, "Between Two and Four': The French Initiative and the Multi-Power Diplomatic Initiatives to Resolve the Middle East Crisis,' *Diplomacy & Statecraft*, vol. 27, no. 1 (2016), pp. 93-120.

199 Humaira Dar, 'Nuclear Diplomacy: A Case Study of French and Pakistani Behaviour,' *Pakistan Vision*, vol. 18, no. 2 (2017), pp. 211-236.

200 Philip T. Hoffman, 'Why Was It Europeans Who Conquered the World?' p. 603.

201 J. W. Young, 'Review article. French Diplomacy,' *History*, vol. 75, issue 245 (October 1990), p. 425.

NATIONAL STYLES IN SCIENCE, DIPLOMACY, AND SCIENCE DIPLOMACY

integration and cooperation, and has given a special meaning to international organisations and the role of diplomacy.

Contemporary French diplomacy puts a greater emphasis on the processes of continuous European integration in which France attempts to play a leadership role. Based on the concept of 'cohabitation', this is a rational policy for France as a country geographically 'squeezed' between other European nations. By contrast, the relative geographical isolation of the British Isles has meant that British foreign policy towards Europe could be more open, making it a diplomacy of possibilities. The Brexit vote can be seen as an example of this.

Being part of the EU imposes another kind of dilemma: France might struggle to find a balance between its own foreign policy objectives and European objectives, especially in areas where the collective sovereignty of the EU might potentially restrict the national interests of member nations.[202] Maintaining 'cohabitation' requires skilful and savvy everyday diplomacy to preserve French national interests within the European cohort.

As an example, US President Donald Trump reportedly asked French President Emmanuel Macron to leave the EU in order to get a better bilateral trade deal with the United States.[203] If true, Macron potentially faced a choice between policy based on French national interest, and policy based on the collective interests of the EU. Since the start of the Fifth Republic, which owes much to Charles de Gaulle's political and diplomatic system, the president retains a critical role in formulating foreign policy. Acknowledging that personal relations between the French president and other state leaders influence French foreign policy,[204] Trump's approach to Macron might not be as opportunistic as it appears, but rather a carefully considered opportunity.

A distinct series of elements of French national diplomatic style no doubt reflect France's historical and contemporary attempts to map out areas of interests and its own place on the European continent and beyond. Due to its historical rivalry with the UK and limited by other major powers, French diplomacy became a 'movement diplomacy' of bold initiatives, and later a rational 'cohabitation diplomacy' showcasing France's enthusiasm for European integration. Aristocratic from the beginning, the French diplomatic corps remains

---

202   David Spence, 'Taking Stock: 50 Years of European Diplomacy,' *The Hague Journal of Diplomacy*, vol. 4 (2009), p. 240.

203   Alina Polyakova & Benjamin Haddad, 'Europe in the New Era of Great Power Competition. How the EU Can Stand Up to Trump and China,' *Foreign Affairs* (17 July, 2018). Available at: https://www.foreignaffairs.com/articles/europe/2018-07-17/europe-new-era-great-power -competition. Accessed 5 August, 2018.

204   Richard Balme, 'Revisiting French diplomacy in the age of globalization,' *French Politics*, vol. 8, no. 1 (2010), p. 93.

a carrier of French culture and social norms to be represented and promoted in foreign countries.

Historical peculiarities and modern geopolitics represent French diplomatic strategy in two more ways, adding an extra element to the country's national style in diplomacy. First, like the British, French diplomacy is mainly consular. Second, French diplomacy limits the involvement or influence of public opinion, reflecting the enormous power of the French president to formulate foreign policy.

To elaborate on the latter, when conducting foreign policy France sees its domestic interests as a priority, and combines French foreign policy with domestic policy-making. However, the interdependency of foreign and domestic policies has brought surprising results that could compromise France's political culture and political institutions, especially if there is a lack of mediation between foreign policy and public opinion.[205] Richard Balme laments that French foreign policy and diplomacy "have very few elements on interactions between social movements, political parties, public opinion, and the conduct of civil diplomacy managing international policy issues such as trade, climate change, financial globalisation or poverty reduction."[206]

I would suggest a slightly more optimistic view than Balme. There is one more element of French diplomacy that seems very progressive and could be taken as the future of French diplomacy – *French scientific and cultural diplomacy*. As a form of soft power, this diplomacy is a primary source for French international influence, and goes some way towards addressing international policy issues and global problems. French scientific and cultural diplomacy, alongside a Realist approach to foreign policy, is a way for France to build strong influence.

5.3   *Scientific and Cultural Diplomacy*

The chronology of French science diplomacy is best summarised in reverse. In 2013, the Ministry of Foreign Affairs published a policy paper titled 'Science Diplomacy for France'. The paper was based on 'National Research and Innovation Strategy' of 2009 issued by the Ministry of Higher Education and Research. The 2009 strategy document can be seen as an embodiment of French science diplomacy, and is itself merely a continuation of the French scientific and cultural diplomacy of 1998, when the country's scientific and cultural networks were merged to tackle the global challenges of economic

---

205   Ibid., p. 94.
206   Ibid., p. 94.

NATIONAL STYLES IN SCIENCE, DIPLOMACY, AND SCIENCE DIPLOMACY 57

and financial regulation, climate, health, education and sustainable growth.[207] French scientific and cultural diplomacy, for its part, is a continuation of *French science policy* from the time of de Gaulle. The progression of this strategy is a strong component of France's national style in science and diplomacy, which is a reflection of the inseparability of the French state and science. The inclusion of culture component became the basis for French foreign policies and their implementation by everyday diplomacy.

Like British science diplomacy, French science diplomacy engages on bilateral and multilateral levels with developed and developing countries, and works to address global issues. Maintaining relations with developed countries fits with both the *diplomacy for science* and *science in diplomacy* dimensions. France is a leader in multinational scientific projects such as CERN and international space cooperation. Scientific cooperation with developed countries is directed towards high-level research projects that require significant funding to support the French standard of academic excellence. France acknowledges that addressing global challenges like health and food security, and contributing to the development of environment and ecological technologies, are a matter of global cooperation and shared responsibility. At the same time, France realistically admits that it must adjust its science and industry to meet global challenges.[208] Science diplomacy and cultural diplomacy are effective tools to help France maintain its position as a major international power.

Strengthening partnerships with the Global South by making use of its cultural and educational reputation is another important component of France's foreign policy. This fits into the *science for diplomacy* dimension. Two-thirds of French overseas offices are located in the Global South, particular in Africa, Asia, and the Middle East. France attaches a critical importance to maintaining a ground presence in its traditional regions of influence.[209] French diplomatic missions push the educational sphere forward when it comes to interstate relations. In particular, France develops a specific policy on scientific cooperation structured around vigilance in science and technology.[210] An exceptional part of the *science for diplomacy* dimension is that it can be used to improve strained bilateral relations or establish contact when a relationship is non-existent.[211] The approach is especially useful in the 'problematic' countries of the Middle East after the Arab Spring, when relations with Western

---

207 Philippe Lane, *French Scientific and Cultural Diplomacy*, p. 17.
208 Alexei V. Shestopal & Nikolay V. Litvak, 'Science Diplomacy: French Experience,' p. 107.
209 Pierre-Bruno Ruffini, *Science and Diplomacy: A New Dimension of International Relations*, p. 51.
210 Philippe Lane, *French Scientific and Cultural Diplomacy*, p. 86.
211 Alexei V. Shestopal & Nikolay V. Litvak, 'Science Diplomacy: French Experience,' p. 109.

countries were challenged, or with almost diplomatically isolated countries like North Korea.

The proclaimed values of scientific culture, public debate, scientific education, and tradition in expertise and research, are the foundation upon which France builds its scientific and cultural diplomacy. These ideas are promoted through the network of French cultural centres and missions abroad, prioritising education and cultural influence. Through all of these, France demonstrates an impressive ability to generate soft power in science diplomacy, which can fairly be called the diplomacy of knowledge.[212] Promoting culture, linguistics, education, and academic activities accord with France's long-term diplomatic strategy. This strategy aligns with French foreign policy, not only in its pragmatic goal of building influence with the major emerging markets of the Global South, but also as a means of providing humanitarian assistance when needed.

When it comes to global governance, the role of French science diplomacy would be rather moderate, given the strained geopolitical circumstances of recent times and the transition towards a multipolar system. However, France's role as a regional stakeholder on the European continent and a leader of European integration is solid and is likely to continue. At the same time, France's traditional influence in the Global South will also be deepened as the country works to capitalise on these emerging markets.

6 The United States

6.1 *American Science*

Rooted in European heritage, America's style in science could not be anything but Western. In general, the core of scientific development is based on the principle of academic freedom, which, it is believed, could only arise from the foundations of liberalism. The roots of liberalism in academic institutions go back to the scientific revolution in Europe, which naturally spread throughout the North Atlantic.

The age of science was a time of American isolationism and a missionary zeal for progress. It was also a time when the country truly emerged and announced itself as a great power.[213] The changes of the first half of the 20th century have created and consolidated America's great power status, and the

---

212 Philippe Lane, *French Scientific and Cultural Diplomacy*, p. 48.

213 David Milne, *Worldmaking: The Art and Science of American Diplomacy* (NY: Farrar, Straus and Giroux, 2017), p. 9.

NATIONAL STYLES IN SCIENCE, DIPLOMACY, AND SCIENCE DIPLOMACY 59

country's scientific and technological development played no small role in this consolidation. This time was also the beginning of American imperialism as the politics of isolationism was put aside.

In the age of global science, when science and technology added a dramatic new dimensions to state power,[214] the US continued to build influence as a strong regional and global leader. During the bipolar rivalry of the Cold War, science played a large role in the competition between the United States and the Soviet Union. America's victory in the Cold War, and the following period of unilateralism it enjoyed, was decided not only by its more efficient economic and political organisation, but also by America's scientific prowess and academic freedom.

America's approach towards science and technology relates to the country's economic development and might be recognised in two core elements: social efficiency, and a balance between the personal and public good. First, Americans have historically had great admiration for the strength of industrial research, innovation, and production. Second, American consumer culture has had a great impact on technological research and development.[215] Industrial research and consumer culture mark America as a large-scale, highly efficient economy. However, these elements could only arise from a strong national educational system and way of doing science.

Loren Graham, a noted historian of science, distinguished several American peculiarities that helped integrate its national values, economy, politics, and scientific development.[216] I adapt these peculiarities to help identify constructive elements of America's national style in science.

First, the strongly legalistic nature of disputes in American society is a cornerstone of American political culture, which indicates the role of public debate and the eagerness of politicians for public approval. This characteristic almost completely prevents political control over academic freedom.

Second, America's national style in science is also shaped by the continuing strength of religious traditions and the belief that it is legitimate for religious viewpoints to influence policymaking. This approach might have been directly related to Britain's religious-based motivations to uncover and understand the nature of 'God's Laws'.

---

214   Joseph Nye, *Soft Power – The Means to Success in World Politics.*

215   Loren R. Graham, *Science in Russia and the Soviet Union. A Short History* (Cambridge University Press, 1993), p. 175.

216   Loren R. Graham, 'When Ideology and Controversy Collide: The Case of Soviet Science,' *The Hastings Center Report*, vol. 12, no. 2 (April 1982), p. 31; Loren R. Graham, 'Big Science in the Last Years of the Big Soviet Union,' *Osiris*, vol. 7 (1992), p. 50.

Third, America's tendency to fund research through contracts and grants to individual chief investigators, rather than provide block-funding to whole institutions, has helped ensure both the efficiency of academic departments and the division between private and public interests. The funding system also gives space to a wide cohort of lobbies, interest groups, and various kinds of professional organisations. America's method of funding research contrasts to the French inseparability between the state and science.

These peculiarities point to some fundamental features of how America's university system is organised. Large American universities are the home of most of the ground-breaking research conducted in the country. The autonomy and continuous competitiveness of American universities, their ongoing competition for funding, and their need to showcase results-oriented projects, are all fertile ground for the development of world-leading theoretical and applied science. Academic autonomy is yet another element of America's national style in science.

In general, America's style in science is based on the efficiency and creativity of various scientific projects. The country's results-oriented science system is applied to both academia and industry. Large universities are where the most significant research is conducted. However, the competition for funding opportunities and results-oriented nature of scientific projects require a balance between the public good, academic freedom and public approval. The greatest strength of America's academic system is its flexibility, which allows the country to maintain a leading position as a global power strengthened by 'forward-deployed diplomacy.'

6.2 *Forward-deployed Diplomacy*

The era of American isolationism arose in the 19th century, at a time when the country felt remarkably secured and confident. America had benefited from its geographic distance from the world's conflicts and other power centres. The country also faced no significant threat from any of its neighbours.[217] America's isolationism existed in harmony with a liberal approach to international politics. This changed following America's acquisition of territories after the Spanish-American War. The country went on to pursue the rhetoric of liberation for former Spanish colonies, declared its Open Door Policy in China, fought against Nazi Germany in World War Two, and then helped

---

217 Thomas Hanson, 'The Traditions and Travails of Career Diplomacy in the United States,' in Paul Sharp and Geoffrey Wiseman (ed.), *American Diplomacy* (Koninklijke Brill NV, Leiden, The Netherlands 2012), p. 200.

NATIONAL STYLES IN SCIENCE, DIPLOMACY, AND SCIENCE DIPLOMACY

rebuild Western Europe.[218] So long as America's foreign policy and diplomacy continued to produce positive results for the country, it was not overly difficult for the government to achieve its democratic goal of ensuring state policies enjoyed popular domestic support.[219]

In the 20th century, the politics of isolationism changed. This by no means put America at a risk or made the country any less confident – quite the opposite. America was affected by changes in the European balance of power and was a driving force for the institutionalised North Atlantic community following World War Two. This opened the pathway for an era of American-led international institutions[220] and global leadership. Washington's leadership might be credited with enabling a relative global peace after 1945.[221]

Given the nature of America's political system, the separation of powers among the president, Congress, and the courts, put foreign policy and diplomacy in a position of 'invitation to struggle' when the role of the Senate in declaring war, passing foreign affairs budgets, ratifying treaties, and approving ambassadorial appointments set clear limits on the executive branch.[222]

American foreign policy and diplomacy are well discussed in academic literature[223] and there is no need for me to recount American grand strategy and its implications here. Instead, I focus on America's national diplomatic style, which may not be a strict reflection of the country's approach to foreign policy but is nevertheless a critical component. The blurred distinction between American foreign policy and diplomacy is notable and is in fact a

---

218   George F. Kennan, *American Diplomacy: Sixtieth-Anniversary Expanded Edition* (The University of Chicago Press, 2012).

219   Ibid., p. 272.

220   David Armitage, 'The Atlantic Ocean' in David Armitage, Alison Bashford & Sujit Sivasundaram (ed.), *Oceanic Histories* (Cambridge University Press, 2018), pp. 92-93.

221   Eliot A. Cohen, *The big Stick. The Limits of Soft Power & the Necessity of Military Force* (New York, NY: Basic Books, 2016), p. 1.

222   George F. Kennan, *American Diplomacy: Sixtieth-Anniversary Expanded Edition*, p. 200.

223   See, for instance, classical works by W. W. Rostow, 'The American National Style,' *Daedalus*, vol. 87, no. 2 (Spring 1958), pp. 110-144; George F. Kennan, *American Diplomacy: Sixtieth-Anniversary Expanded Edition* (The US: The University of Chicago Press, 2012); Henry Kissinger, *Diplomacy* (New York, NY: Simon & Schuster, 1994); Paul Sharp & Geoffrey Wiseman (ed.), *American Diplomacy* (Koninklijke Brill NV, Leiden, The Netherlands, 2012); Henry Kissinger, *World* Order (Penguin Books, 2015); Joseph S. Nye, *Is the American Century Over?* (The UK: Polity Press, 2015); David Milne, *Worldmaking: The Art and Science of American Diplomacy* (NY: Farrar, Straus and Giroux, 2017); Richard Haass, *A World in Disarray: American Foreign Policy and the Crisis of the Old Order: American Foreign Policy and the Crisis of the Old Order* (Penguin Books, 2018).

critical element of America's style of diplomacy. Despite this, the distinction between the two has been largely neglected in academic literature.[224]

American foreign policy and diplomacy have traditionally gone hand-in-hand. The formulation, understanding, and use of both foreign policy and diplomacy, in theory and practice, have been largely interchangeable. This has meant that diplomats themselves have made and implemented foreign policy. Diplomats use analytical insight, play intelligence roles, and ultimately build up knowledge about the countries in which they are posted. When diplomats complete their service, they quite often remain in their countries of residence, becoming analysts or consultants of the nations they have experience dealing with. In general, diplomats have been and continue to be source of America's foreign policy initiatives.

The importance of professional training for diplomats was formulated by George Kennan, a top American diplomat and academic. Kennan emphasised the role of career diplomats to create and initiate foreign policy. Properly trained career diplomats are meant to become professionals in the conduct of foreign policy[225] and maintain a balance of power based on the system of democracy.[226] This tight bond between diplomacy and foreign policy can be taken as a main feature of America's diplomatic style. America differs here from Britain, France and Russia, where diplomacy is the implementation of state foreign policy formulated by the government or a state leader.

Another characteristic of America's diplomatic style lies in the integration of foreign policy academics and practitioners. For instance, the two most notable American ambassadors to Moscow are the above-mentioned George Kennan, and Michael McFaul, who served in Russia more than half a century afterwards. Both became leading scholars and distinguished academics of their respective generations as foreign policy analysts and Russia specialists. George Kennan's decades-long professorship at Princeton, and Michael McFaul's current professorship at Stanford, certainly indicate a great freedom for returning diplomats to share their understanding of American foreign policy and diplomacy to a wide audience. The autonomy of American universities allows for this. The integration of theory and practice is one of the great strengths of American foreign policy and diplomacy.

Geoffrey Wiseman writes that America's diplomatic culture and practices are distinct from those of other countries. He suggests seven interconnected

---

224 Geoffrey Wiseman, 'Pax Americana: Bumping into Diplomatic culture,' *International Studies Perspectives*, vol. 6, (2005), p. 410.

225 George F. Kennan, *American Diplomacy: Sixtieth-Anniversary Expanded Edition*, p. 100.

226 Ibid., p. 78.

NATIONAL STYLES IN SCIENCE, DIPLOMACY, AND SCIENCE DIPLOMACY

characteristics of American diplomacy, which might contradict to my own perspective when it comes to the theoretical and practical integration of American diplomacy. I list them all here to better clarify my own analysis.

These characteristics are:

1) America's long-held distrust and negative view of diplomats and diplomacy, which has contributed to the historical neglect and side-lining of the US Department of State in America's policy-making process;

2) a high degree of domestic influence over foreign policy and diplomacy;

3) a tendency to privilege hard power over soft power in foreign policy;

4) a preference for bilateral over multilateral diplomacy;

5) an ideological tradition of diplomatically isolating states that are considered adversarial and of refusing to engage them until they meet preconditions;

6) a tradition of appointing a relatively high proportion of political rather than career ambassadors;

7) a demonstrably strong cultural disposition towards a direct, low-context negotiating style.[227]

Characteristics 1, 2, and 6, in particular, contradict my view that American diplomacy and foreign policy is highly successful and is made by professional diplomats. Nonetheless, I would not underestimate the extent to which the structural approach towards US diplomacy and foreign policymaking is disappearing. One might say that the change in diplomacy, even with a negative view of diplomacy, is a sign of a broader transformation that reflects internal and external alterations. Characteristics 3, 5, and 7 are in line with the hawkish Realism of American foreign policy. Finally, characteristic 4 might be justifiable in traditional diplomacy but would not disadvantageous in science diplomacy given America's attitude toward international collaboration.

Washington's leadership and the role of professional diplomats in pursuing the long-lasting peace are also challenged by practitioners. The reason lies in not only the political climate of the Trump administration, but also the determination of external forces – in particular the rise of Asian powers.

Two recently published memoirs by former State Department officials, James Dobbins[228] and Ronan Farrow,[229] express nostalgia for the 'good old times' – times when career diplomats played a valued role in formulating and

---

227 Geoffrey Wiseman, 'Distinctive Characteristics of American Diplomacy,' *The Hague Journal of Diplomacy*, vol. 6 (2011), pp. 235-259.

228 James Dobbins, *Foreign Service: Five Decades on the Frontlines of American Diplomacy*, (Washington D.C.: Brookings Institution Press, 2017).

229 Ronan Farrow, *War on Peace: The End of Diplomacy and the Decline of American Influence*, (New York, London: W.W. Norton, 2018).

implementing American foreign policy on the cutting edge of interstate inter-actions, and when the US enjoyed global leadership. Farrow would likely agree with Wiseman about the neglect of American diplomacy, but argues that "side-lining diplomacy is not an inevitability of global change, it is a choice, made again and again by administrations Democratic and Republican."[230]

Indeed, the 2017 National Security Strategy[231] pays little attention to tradi-tional diplomacy, not to mention the absence of science diplomacy. Instead it strongly recommends that diplomats pursue a 'forward-deployed' type of field-work to advance and defend America's national interests abroad. Diplomats are strongly recommended to facilitate people-to-people exchanges, build networks, and lead coalitions, with a goal of promoting economic diplomacy (a high priority) and American values. The Strategy also affirms that a strong military is needed to allow diplomats to operate from a position of strength.[232]

America's increasingly militarised approach to foreign policy is also noted by Farrow. He emphasises that this approach marks a continuity of American foreign policy between Trump and his predecessors, as part of a shift from soft to hard power since 9/11.[233] The assertive character of American for-eign policy is also stressed by David Milne, who argues that such policy goes along "with necessary wars, adroit alliance building, Pyrrhic economic and political victories, the maladroit use of the CIA, [and] reckless foreign-policy misadventures."[234] America's militarised approach and its containment strat-egy to balance great powers fits perfectly into Realist theory, leaving space for Liberalism only in rhetoric. American state policy itself has been guided by Realist logic, "although the public pronouncements of its leaders might lead one to think otherwise."[235]

In sum, key elements of America's style in diplomacy might appear contra-dictory when encountering the Realist implications of foreign policy – foreign policy which is safeguarded by military capacity with professional diplomacy born of decades of experience. The experience is derived from the propensity and flexibility of individuals to restrict the whims of ambitious politicians. This

---

230   Ibid., p. 35.

231   'National Security Strategy of the United States of America,' The White House (December 2017). Available at: https://www.whitehouse.gov/wp-content/uploads/2017/12/NSS-Final -12-18-2017-0905.pdf. Accessed 8 August 2018.

232   'National Security Strategy of the United States of America.'

233   Ronan Farrow, *War on Peace: The End of Diplomacy and the Decline of American Influence*, p. 148.

234   David Milne, *Worldmaking: The Art and Science of American Diplomacy*, p. 18.

235   John J. Mearsheimer, *The Tragedy of Great Powers Politics* (New York, NY: W.W. Norton & Company, 2001), p. 94.

NATIONAL STYLES IN SCIENCE, DIPLOMACY, AND SCIENCE DIPLOMACY 65

kind of restriction, however, might be disastrous for American foreign policy, as Farrow notes, and could lead to the State Department suffering a loss of power with little counterbalance from civilian voices.[236] Finally, propagating American values creates a strong tendency towards American exceptionalism. This has ethical implications when America, a country that sees itself as the vanguard of liberal democracy and global prosperity, makes moral judgements on the behaviour of other states.[237]

6.3 *A Science Diplomacy Leader*

Along with Britain, America is a trendsetter in contemporary science diplomacy and takes the lead in each recognised dimension of it. The Trump administration seems to underestimate the country's involvement in global issues[238] and de-emphasises the contributions of science and scientists to the country's detriment when negotiating on global climate change.[239] Despite this, science diplomacy might be one of the most efficient and promising tools for America's forward-deployed diplomacy. American science diplomacy is also a solid foundation for global governance. Before I outline my arguments to support this, some historical context might be helpful. There are many examples where America, by utilising scientists and their knowledge, was able to gain benefits from cooperating with others that it could not have gained alone. For instance, in the German-American Pork War of 1880-1891, the International Geophysical Year of 1956-1957, and the Montreal Protocol of 1987,[240] science and the scientific community played a sizeable role in devising and carrying out foreign policy and diplomacy.

During the Cold War, the foreign policy goals of the two superpowers required diplomatic multitasking. Both America and the Soviet Union practiced science diplomacy to achieve the goal of spreading influence in the Third World, by helping underdeveloped countries to eradicate deadly diseases. Such

---

236 Ronan Farrow, *War on Peace: The End of Diplomacy and the Decline of American Influence*, p. 396.

237 George F. Kennan, *American Diplomacy: Sixtieth-Anniversary Expanded Edition*, p. 107.

238 See for instance a running list of US science and environmental policy in which the US was deliberately withdrawn by the initiative of the Trump administration: National Geographic, 'A Running List of How Trump Is Changing the Environment,' 16 March, 2018. Available at: https://news.nationalgeographic.com/2017/03/how-trump-is-changing-science-environment/. Accessed 10 August 2018.

239 Elizabeth L. Chalecki, 'Knowledge in Sheep's Clothing: How Science Informs American Diplomacy,' *Diplomacy & Statecraft*, vol. 19, no. 1 (2017), p. 1.

240 Ibid., pp. 1-19.

was the case for vaccine diplomacy.[241] Reinforcing bilateral relations with each other, both adversaries went through at least a decade-long project of space diplomacy.[242] They also participated in international scientific exploration of the Antarctic and used it as a advantage in the rivalry for territory.[243]

The story of how science diplomacy become an important part of American foreign policy begins from the American tradition of public engagement within its political system. Science diplomacy can be considered a part of public diplomacy, as America's wide range of non-state actors and their energetic involvement in 'country-making' and 'world-making' has opened up traditional diplomacy to various public initiatives. Science diplomacy is one of these public initiatives. As an example, the American Association for the Advancement of Science co-authored a widely cited report on science diplomacy in 2010.[244] Thus, like America's diplomatic style, the country's national style in science diplomacy is characterised by the ability of individuals and institutions to influence policymakers.

American science diplomacy is a part of American public diplomacy. As a response to Soviet propaganda, in 1953 the US established the United States Information Agency (USIA). The Agency was operational until 1999 and was a prototype for America's modern public diplomacy. Since the end of the Cold War, the USIA's role has evolved into addressing first the threat of Islamic terrorism and more recently the 'sharp power' of Chinese and Russian information warfare.[245] In contrast to the violence of propaganda, public diplomacy is non-violent; forms partnerships with the education sector, for which the US is a world leader; takes longer to engage with audiences; and ultimately has better long-term outcomes. Public diplomacy is an unobtrusive reminder of the difference between America and other powers, as it stands in contrasts with

---

241 Erez Manela, 'A Pox on Your Narrative: Writing Disease Control into Cold War History,' *Diplomatic History*, vol. 34, no. 2 (April 2010), pp. 299-323; Peter J. Hotez, 'Russian–United States Vaccine Science Diplomacy: Preserving the Legacy', *PLoS Negl Trop Dis*, 11(5): e0005320; Peter J. Hotez, '"Vaccine Diplomacy": Historical Perspectives and Future Directions', *PLoS Negl Trop Dis*, 8(6): e2808.

242 Olga Krasnyak, 'The Apollo-Soyuz Test Project: Construction of an Ideal Type of Science Diplomacy,' *The Hague Journal of Diplomacy*, vol. 13, no. 4 (2018), pp. 1-2; Edward Clinton Ezell & Linda Neuman Ezell, *The Partnership, a History of the Apollo-Soyuz Test Project* (The US: NASA, 1978).

243 Elizabeth L. Chalecki, 'Knowledge in Sheep's Clothing: How Science Informs American Diplomacy,' p. 7.

244 The AAAS & the Royal Society, 'New frontiers in science diplomacy' (2010).

245 Joseph S. Nye Jr., 'How Sharp Power Threatens Soft Power,' *Foreign Affairs* (24 January, 2018). Available at: https://www.foreignaffairs.com/articles/china/2018-01-24/how-sharp -power-threatens-soft-power?cid=nlc-fa_fatoday-20180124. Accessed 10 August 2018.

the diplomatic approaches of both Russian propaganda and Chinese 'sharp' power.

Even though the objectives of public diplomacy differ from those of science diplomacy, both types of diplomacy place an enormous importance on public debate and audience engagement. The relationship between public diplomacy and science diplomacy also lies within soft power approaches. America's ability to generate soft power through science diplomacy is immense, and makes it one of the most scientifically attractive countries in the world. Scientific attractiveness includes many factors, among them the quality of the education system. As evidence, America successfully attracts hundreds of thousands of students from all around the world and has done so for decades. Scientific attractiveness also includes opportunities for start-up projects and entrepreneurship. The strength of American research universities constantly attracts international scholars and has seen America receive far more Nobel Prizes than any other nations.[246] All of this together gives American science diplomacy great potential to strengthen and grow, despite temporary political uncertainties.

America's understanding and practical implementation of science diplomacy as part of its foreign policy and diplomacy might be considered the basis for global governance, international collaboration and shared responsibility. The tradition of transparency through public debate is a valuable characteristic for global governance, and America's political system has great potential to fit into this role.

However, the ideas of American exceptionalism and the superiority of American values,[247] historically rooted from classical liberal ideology, might be an obstacle. Even though Liberalism as a broad ideology has shown itself to have great longevity, understandings of Liberalism are as varied as the number of states in which its ideas have been adopted. America's self-declared exceptionalism and superiority would certainly be challenged by other nations. In this regard, promoting a rules-based liberal order and ridding itself of ideas of superiority and exceptionalism might be prudent pathway towards global governance with American leadership.

America is no doubt a front-runner in modern science diplomacy. The intellectual and personified character of American diplomacy and the work of diplomats might soften the assertive and militarised aspects of American

---

246   Loren R. Graham, *Science in Russia and the Soviet Union. A Short History* (Cambridge University Press, 1993), p. 202.

247   John J. Mearsheimer, 'Introduction' in George F. Kennan, *American Diplomacy: Sixtieth-Anniversary Expanded Edition* (The University of Chicago Press 2012), p. 40.

foreign policy. They might even reduce the rhetoric of exceptionalism and superiority. An advanced educational model, highly developed science and technology, and then liberal traditions of public diplomacy – taken together, these are the essential elements of America's national style in science diplomacy.

7   Russia

7.1   *The Russian Century of Science*
The history of modern science in Russia started from Peter the Great, who was an advocate for North European civilisation and its achievements and intentionally imported European science to the country. Peter the Great aimed for Russia to catch up with European civilisation and its scientific progress at that time, while also developing relations between Russia and advanced European nations. By the 19th century, while Russia had not yet become an obvious scientific adversary of Britain and France, its connections to the European scientific community were firmly in place. Russia's scientific community was therefore partly European, and the country's scientific establishment ranked just below its counterparts in Europe.[248]

Russian science was part of state policy to attract European researches, explorers, and adventurers. Such people were granted privileges and citizenship and contributed to Russia's scientific progress and imperial ambitions. The number of skilled foreign academics and professionals who were willing to serve, work, and do research in Russia, while not massive, was still notable, and was used effectively in statecraft, diplomacy, and science. European explorers and scientists who entered the Russian Navy, the Russian Army, and the Imperial Academy of Sciences, became official Russian explorers and scientists, yet in practice were the carriers of European education, values, standards, culture, and traditions. These people complied with the requirements and aspirations of progress and in many cases imported into Russia fundamental scientific knowledge and vital practical skills.

Science might have been a foreign import, yet it was one that took exceptionally well to Russian soil.[249] Russia's substantial transformation in social

---

248   Loren R. Graham, *Science in Russia and the Soviet Union. A Short History*, p. 32.

249   Michael D. Gordin, 'The Heidelberg Circle: German Inflections on the Professionalisation of Russian Chemistry in the 1860s,' in Michael Gordin, Karl Hall & Alexei Kojevnikov (ed.), *Intelligentsia Science: The Russian Century, 1860-1960, Osiris*, Second Series, vol. 23 (Chicago: The University of Chicago Press 2008), p. 24.

NATIONAL STYLES IN SCIENCE, DIPLOMACY, AND SCIENCE DIPLOMACY 69

institutions and scientific progress led to the phenomenon of *Russian science* and the 'Russian century' as the country started making its own scientific achievements.[250] The *age of science* and *age of global science* categories might not strictly apply to Russia but are embedded into the Russian century, which lasted from 1860 to the 1960s. The Russian century is the period of assimilation and adaptation of European scientific traditions and institutions into Russian culture and an era in which the country developed its own national science.

Understanding the Russian century requires us to acknowledge the phenomenon of *intelligentsia*. The term *intelligentsia* refers to a heterogeneous and evolving social institution, a useful historical category when analysing the role of the educated elite in Russia and the Soviet Union. The *intelligentsia* of the 19th century was an oppositional movement who criticised, guided, and led the shaping of Russian culture, politics and society, ultimately bringing about Western-style then liberalisation of the country. While even the libertarians lacked the ability to radically change Russian traditional society, the development of science was secured by the state's power, as science strengthened the state in return. The *intelligentsia* was also influential at the beginning of the 20th century, bringing about the Bolshevik Revolution and turning a page of world history. The *intelligentsia* phenomenon is an element of Russia's national style in science.

In the first part of the Russian century, Russian science progressed in the natural sciences, anthropology, and ethnography, all of which were highly influenced by British science and the Darwinian concept of evolution. The school of chemistry was brought across from the southern German states, particularly from the University of Heidelberg, and was then well developed in Russia.[251] A scientific pedagogy then grew on Russia's home soil, giving rise to social sciences in the country.[252] Prior to the development of space technologies, and driven not by the belief in the power of science and technology but by philosophical traditions associated with the mystical occult tradition, Cosmism emerged in Russia.[253] Cosmism, one of the distinctive elements

---

250 Michael D. Gordin and Karl Hall, 'Introduction: Intelligentsia Science inside and outside Russia,' in Michael Gordin, Karl Hall and Alexei Kojevnikov (ed.), *Intelligentsia Science: The Russian Century, 1860-1960*, p. 11.

251 Michael D. Gordin, 'The Heidelberg Circle: German Inflections on the Professionalisation of Russian Chemistry in the 1860s,' p. 23.

252 Andy Byford, 'Turning Pedagogy into a Science: Teachers and Psychologists in Late Imperial Russia (1897-1917),' in Michael Gordin, Karl Hall and Alexei Kojevnikov (ed.), *Intelligentsia Science: The Russian Century, 1860-1960*, p. 50.

253 Asif A. Siddiqi, 'Imagining the Cosmos: Utopians, Mystics, and the Popular Culture of Spaceflight in Revolutionary Russia,' in Michael Gordin, Karl Hall and Alexei Kojevnikov (ed.), *Intelligentsia Science: The Russian Century, 1860-1960*, p. 260.

of Russian philosophical thought, was deeply rooted in Russian culture. It is based upon the idea of liberation from death, which was thought to be achievable through human migration into space and the reanimation of atom-like particles.[254] Cosmism is an essential part of the historical roots of Russia's space exploration and eventual leading position in mathematics and theoretical physics.

In the Soviet times, science was under the very close political control of Marxism-Leninism and followed the pathway of its materialistic doctrine in building a strong industrial and military profile.[255] This profile was meant to ensure Russia's position as one of the two superpowers in the bipolar world. Materialism influenced the Soviet style in sciences, and saw man as a physical and biological, rather than social, object.[256] As a result, the social sciences were largely left aside. The Soviet expertise in space technologies was profound, as was Soviet fundamental research in the usage of nuclear and atomic technology.[257]

The ideological interference of the Cold War was disastrous for Soviet science. The pressure to conform with state ideology and the difficulty of innovating under close political control could be what caused Soviet science to eventually stagnate. Centralised planning does not work in science; political freedom, organisational diversity, and diverse methodological approaches – characteristics all present in American science – are essentials for scientific creativity. The Soviet *intelligentsia* might have been a force for independent free thinking in the country, but that was not enough on a nation-wide scale. The Russian century in science was over before the end of the Cold War.

In contemporary Russia, scientific development has mostly declined, although has remained stable in the theoretical sciences. Even now, Russians scientists distinguished by good theoretical training often move to scientifically advanced countries and international institutions, leaving to a massive 'brain drain' in Russia.[258]

---

254   Asif A. Siddiqi, 'Competing Technologies, National(ist) Narratives, and Universal Claims: Toward a Global History of Space Exploration,' *Technology and Culture*, vol. 51, no. 2 (April 2010), p. 432.

255   Loren R. Graham, 'When Ideology and Controversy Collide: The Case of Soviet Science,' *The Hastings Center Report*, vol. 12, no. 2 (April, 1982), p. 26.

256   Ibid., p. 27.

257   Sonja D. Schmid, 'Organisational Culture and Professional Identities in the Soviet Nuclear Power Industry,' in Michael Gordin, Karl Hall and Alexei Kojevnikov (ed.), *Intelligentsia Science: The Russian Century, 1860-1960*, p. 82.

258   K. A. Ibragimova & O. N. Barabanov, 'About the Prospects of the Russian Science Diplomacy,' *Vestnik RFFI* [Russian Foundation for Basic Research Herald], no. 1 (97), January-March 2018, p. 58.

NATIONAL STYLES IN SCIENCE, DIPLOMACY, AND SCIENCE DIPLOMACY 71

In brief, the early adoption of modern European science brought a unique form of scientific development on Russian soil. The Russian century was characterised by the predominance of theoretical sciences, foundational mathematics, theoretical physics, and chemistry, while the social sciences and humanities were reflected in the development of philosophical Cosmism. The areas of mathematics and theoretical physics were always strong in Russia,[259] but political control and centralised planning in the Soviet state put the Russian century to an end, leaving contemporary Russia trailing scientifically advanced countries.

Acknowledging the history and recognising the important elements constituting Russia's national style in science help us understand that Russia's re-emergence as a scientific power has a solid foundation. Russian scientists, alongside independent and free-thinking intellectuals (namely the *intelligentsia*), were able to keep Russia on the track of a major power and make the country a valuable player in science diplomacy initiatives. The strength and skilfulness of Russia's traditional diplomacy, backed up by the country's military and nuclear capability, secures Russia's position as a regional stakeholder and helps explain its assertive foreign policy when it comes to territorial acquisition.

7.2 *Network Diplomacy*

Together with importing science into the country, Peter the Great also adopted Europe's diplomatic model, primarily the Swedish and Prussian variants. Russia's standards for diplomacy were taken from the European style of protocol regulations, diplomatic rankings, and even a fashion code for diplomats, allowing the Russian envoys to consider themselves full members of the European diplomatic corps.[260] Russia's national diplomatic style was therefore similar to that of Europe. The number of Russian diplomats by the end of the 19th century was relatively small, perhaps numbering only about 500, which was around 0.5 per cent of the state bureaucracy.[261]

Russian diplomats were part of the aristocratic establishment and were on top of the hierarchy of the country's imperial bureaucratic system. Their distinctive personal qualities and attributes included: having appropriate manners; being proficient in one or more foreign languages; and having

---

259 Loren R. Graham, 'Big Science in the Last Years of the Big Soviet Union,' *Osiris*, vol. 7 (1992), p. 62.

260 Tatiana Zonova, 'Diplomatic Cultures: Comparing Russia and the West in Terms of a 'Modern Model of Diplomacy,' pp. 14, 19.

261 Alexandr Kuznetsov, "Inheriting legends sanctified by the time ...' From the history of the Russian foreign policy doctrine,' *Politia*, no. 4 (2004), p. 2, (in Russian).

written a number of works in literature, history, geography, economics, theology, foreign affairs, international law, and travel. Such attributes made them the best career diplomats. A feature of the diplomatic corps of the 19th century was its selection of refined and well-educated individuals. The diplomatic culture of imperial Russia was a reflection of the Russian culture as a whole. The exceptionalism and excellence of diplomats is an element of national diplomatic style that has been consistently maintained throughout Russia's history, including through the Soviet times and up to the present era.[262]

Much like their British and French counterparts, Russian diplomats were not supposed to formulate foreign policy strategy – that was the prerogative of the emperor or the ruling political regime – but to implement foreign policy. However, the perceptions and viewpoints of diplomats serving abroad, based as they were on their everyday diplomatic practice and above all their personal qualities, were usually well received and considered in formulating foreign policy strategy.

Right after the Bolshevik Revolution, the new leadership viewed diplomacy as a tool for spreading and promoting a Soviet model of the state. When hope for internationalism and the world revolution failed, Soviet diplomacy was soon pragmatically tasked to simply secure the country's national interests. Soviet diplomats worked to fulfil the challenging goal of connecting Soviet Russia with other states and nations. The post-World War Two period and the tensions of the Cold War demanded exceptional negotiations with former and new allies as well as the ability to strengthen Soviet influence globally. *Realpolitik* compelled Soviet diplomacy to take into consideration the alignment of forces and to strive for a balance of power and a nuclear balance of fear.[263] Soviet diplomats were highly competent in pursuing the country's foreign policy objectives, however, the exceptionalism of diplomats also has its downside. Non-state actors and a wider audience were usually restricted from foreign policy debates, and the secrecy of diplomacy was to be protected from any interrogation.

The fall of the Soviet Union and the loss of prestige as a superpower, however, did not change the behaviour of Russian diplomats, who mainly follow the routine patterns of diplomatic practices. The main direction of Russian foreign policy, and therefore a matter of enforcement by diplomats, has had to do with the territory of the former Soviet Union, which is seen as a privileged sphere

---

262   A. I. Ismailov & K. K. Bazarbayev, 'History and Traditions of Russian Diplomacy,' *Historical Sciences*, no. 6 (2012), p. 5, (in Russian).

263   Tatiana Zonova, 'Diplomatic Cultures: Comparing Russia and the West in Terms of a 'Modern Model of Diplomacy," p. 21.

NATIONAL STYLES IN SCIENCE, DIPLOMACY, AND SCIENCE DIPLOMACY

of Russian influence. This has led to a military conflict with Georgia in 2008, the annexation of Crimea in 2014, threats to the Baltic states, and attempts to address Russia's vital security concerns in the Eurasian region, including by limiting the eastward expansion of NATO and the EU.[264] Following this strategy, Russia's diplomatic style appears coercive and confident, with a hawkish *Realist* orientation. The controversy of Russian foreign policy has put the country in a position of relative isolation from the West (examples include Russia's exclusion from the Group of 8 and worsening relations with the US and the UK), has and affected diplomats who often are the target of expulsions and various tit-for-tat actions.

Another fundamental aspect of Russia's diplomatic style is that economic and financial power has almost always been secondary to political power in the country. Russian leaders exclusively determine foreign policy directions while diplomats are seen as merely effective tools to fulfil the government's will. Put simply, traditional diplomacy is a top-down form of decision-making with a high level of formality and secrecy.[265] Russia's style in diplomacy reflects this leadership style. For example, in the 1990s, under the Boris Yeltsin presidency, Russia pursued a more Western-oriented direction based on liberal values and the rules-based order. Since the 2000s, under Putin's leadership, Russian diplomacy has acquired a muscular, multilateral and assertive posture.[266] Officially at least, Russian diplomacy advocates for rational economic and humanitarian cooperation with the West, is against any confrontation, and sees itself a key player in a new global equilibrium.[267]

Russia understands that 'soft' or 'smart' power and non-material capabilities are needed to promote Russia's interests worldwide. This purely pragmatic realisation is represented in 'network diplomacy' rather than in public diplomacy. For Russia, network diplomacy aligns with the primary goal of restraining American dominance and working towards a more balanced, multipolar system.[268] In Russia's view, that can be achieved through building coalitions, face-to-face interactions, and personal relations with top diplomats and state leaders. Russia's network diplomacy also includes an information campaign

---

264 Charles E. Ziegler, 'Diplomacy' in Andrei P. Tsygankov (ed.), *Routledge Handbook of Russian Foreign Policy* (New York, NY: Routledge 2018), p. 124.

265 Vincent Pouliot, *International Security in Practice: The Politics of NATO-Russia Diplomacy* (UK, Cambridge: Cambridge University Press, 2010), pp. 134-138.

266 Charles E. Ziegler, 'Diplomacy,' p. 123.

267 Sergey Lavrov, 'Russia's Foreign Policy in a Historical Perspective,' Russia in Global Affairs (20 March 2018). Available at: http://eng.globalaffairs.ru/number/Russias-Foreign-Policy-in-a-Historical-Perspective-19445. Accessed 10 July, 2018.

268 Charles E. Ziegler, 'Diplomacy,' p. 132.

to significantly shape international information influence[269] while constructing an information climate preferable for Russia. Together with informational warfare, there also exist more neutral public organisations that promote the Russian language and the country's classical cultural heritage.

The accessibility of communication technologies and their practical use, for instance, in social media, affects Russia's diplomatic style. The practices of cyber, informational, and hybrid warfare that are in the use by some Russian embassies abroad create an atmosphere of distrust and suspicion. So long as the ethical reasoning behind these innovations is question by the international community, information warfare and related practices have a counter-productive impact on Russia's national diplomatic style. The research on information warfare and the role of Russian embassies in conducting it, as well as the effect on diplomatic practices, falls under the remit of digital diplomacy, not science diplomacy. However, omitting these contemporary destructive practices from analysis would make it difficult to fully comprehend Russia's diplomatic style.

To summarise, Russia's diplomatic style is pragmatic, Realist, non-ideological, tailored solely to the defence and promotion of Russian state interests (preferably without resort to force), and aims to avoid isolation and preserve an international balance of power favourable to Russia's interests. The professionalism and careful selection of Russian diplomats has a long history, making it a privilege to have a career in diplomatic service. Network diplomacy is a main element of Russia's national diplomatic style, yet utilising communication techniques for informational warfare has a negative effect on the country's diplomatic influence, making its diplomacy appear more like propaganda than a genuine attempt to engage with other nations.

7.3 *Embracing the Potential of Science Diplomacy*

During the Cold War, the Soviet Union demonstrated highly engaged and effective practices of science diplomacy. All dimensions of the science diplomacy taxonomy were well utilised: using science to improve and maintain bilateral relations; providing broad international scientific cooperation in multinational projects; and leading the way in the formulation and elaboration of various international treaties, agreements, and declarations. The Soviet Union's cohesive military hard power, scientific capability and wide diplomatic network contributed to its science diplomacy immensely. The Cold War rivalry

---

269 Dmitry Sivovolov, 'The Role of Russian Diplomacy in the Construction of 'Electronic Government' in Russia,' *MGIMO Review on International Relations*, [Vestrnik MGIMO] vol. 5 (32) (2013), p. 54, (in Russian).

NATIONAL STYLES IN SCIENCE, DIPLOMACY, AND SCIENCE DIPLOMACY 75

was marked not only by serious competition but also frequent cooperation between the two ideological blocks. The success of Russia's vaccine diplomacy and space diplomacy with the US speaks for itself.

Contemporary Russia recognises the importance of science diplomacy but is lacking in the areas of implementation and relevant academic research.[270] Russia's practice of science diplomacy is inconsistent and has critical limitations. On the one hand, the effectiveness of traditional diplomacy and Russia's significant previous scientific achievements contribute to the country's national pride. On the other hand, the current stagnation or even decline in Russian science, the absence of competitive scientific achievements, poor financial support, a struggling national economy, and political constraints, all adversely affect Russia's representation as a scientifically advanced country. Since the collapse of the Soviet Union, Russia's scientific community has also suffered by a brain drain, as scientists leave the country to seek more appealing research opportunities elsewhere.

Another problem for Russia's modern science diplomacy revolves around the involvement of non-state actors in diplomacy and foreign policy-making, which runs against the grain of professional diplomacy. Russia's well-established system of professional training in its foreign service has meant that its diplomats have broad spheres of competency and responsibility. This creates an obstacle for the implementation of science diplomacy. It is not because scientists are unable to advise or be part of traditional diplomacy, but because the participation of non-state actors requires transparency. The openness and publicity of contemporary science diplomacy would present a challenge for Russia's traditional secret diplomacy. Science diplomacy in modern Russia is rather neglected, but there is still considerable potential for things to improve.

Based on the *hypotheses of state behaviour*, Russia might implement science diplomacy in its foreign policy under several scenarios:

- Russia might reflect on the Soviet experience of national self-sufficiency based on the country's existing scientific expertise, human capital, and availability of natural resources. Should the country decide to return down the path towards self-reliance, this would open up opportunities for science diplomacy, particularly *science for diplomacy*, in which scientific contact through people-to-people interactions are used to improve bilateral relations with key international partners.
- Russia's compliance with international treaties, for instance treaties on the Arctic, Antarctic, disarmament and non-proliferation, as well as its

---

270   M. D. Romanova, 'Science Diplomacy: Dimensions and Practices,' *Science, Innovation, Education* [Nauka, Innovatsii, Obrazovanie], no. 1 (23) 2017, pp. 38-52, (in Russian).

participation in international scientific projects like the International Space Station, allow Russia to retain its position as a reliable partner for other nations. In this case, the *science in diplomacy* and *diplomacy in science* dimensions might ensure Russia's role as a regional power. Otherwise, if Russia continues to be overshadowed by its Western partners, this might lead to the destabilisation of existing scientific partnerships.

– If Russia intends to remain a stakeholder in the former Soviet territories, my proposed *science diplomacy for global governance* approach suggests that Russia's movements towards global governance would be more likely to be in rhetoric only rather than a real posture. Moscow's contributions to global governance to date have been marginal, or even obstructive, in response to global governance initiatives by America and Europe.[271] Any attempt to declare global governance or dominance would more likely indicate Moscow's willingness to avoid international isolation and its preference to be identified as an equal partner.

– Russia's stake in science diplomacy may continue in line with a rationale based on hard power and military capability. Amid scientific stagnation, Russia could maintain its geopolitical influence through work in the theoretical sciences, the continuation of academic traditions in higher education, and by making use of wide diplomatic networks. However, Russia lacks the ability in science diplomacy to generate the *soft power* of attraction, due to its internal economic and political hurdles, assertive foreign policy and coercive diplomacy.

– A reliance on traditional diplomacy makes it difficult for non-state actors to be involved in Russia's diplomatic negotiations. Non-state actors (and public opinion in general) have almost no effect in correcting or shaping Russia's foreign policy direction, because that is considered the solely prerogative of the state leadership. Russia's Foreign Ministry might be responsible for implementation but lacks autonomy in policy-making.[272]

In short, Russia lacks the ability to embrace modern science diplomacy on either bilateral or multilateral levels, let alone utilise science diplomacy for global governance purposes. That being said, Russia is receptive to the science diplomacy initiatives of other major powers, with the UK-Russia Year of Science and Education serving as an example. Russia should be seen as a reliable partner to maintain its existing multinational scientific projects and international treaties. If Russia does one day moves to embrace science

---

271   Charles E. Ziegler, 'Diplomacy,' p. 124.

272   Yelena Biberman, 'The Politics of Diplomatic Service Reforms in Post-Soviet Russia,' *Political Science Quarterly*, vol. 126, no. 4, (2011), pp. 669-680.

diplomacy, we will be better able to understand and foresee the consequences if we acknowledging Russia's historical circumstances in which its national style in science and diplomacy was formed.

8 China

8.1 *A Non-Western Power*

China's historical and cultural development strongly contrasts the Western experience. The usual suggested periodisation of science and diplomacy can hardly be applied to China. For our purposes, when looking at the differences between the West and China we should first consider people's mindsets, ways of thinking, and patterns of human behaviour. Under an assumption that looking for Chinese similarities with the West might not prove fruitful, I look instead to axioms of difference. The civilisational roots of Western nations emerged from the European Christendom. In contrast, China's civilisational roots comes from the syncretism of Buddhism, Taoism, Confucianism, and other religious-philosophical categories. While historical and cultural roots evolve, they ultimately tend to preserve patterns reflected in human behaviour, cultural traditions, and community standards.

The question of civilisational difference should be discussed within the fields of philosophy, literature, history, and other humanitarian disciplines. However, I would only note that when making any comparison in national style, acknowledging civilisational differences is a necessity, while Chinese behaviour should not be shoehorned into Western traditions. I limit myself to periodising China's modern science and diplomacy through historical watershed events. While extracting a series of elements characterising China's national style in science and diplomacy will inevitably be somewhat superficial, I attempt to do so in order to identify civilisational differences in national styles.

Contemporary China is rapidly modernising and advancing in many spheres, demonstrating the country's economic and technological progress. If China's outer shell is recognisable to the West, then its internal essence is more likely to remain the preserve of traditional Chinese characteristics that were cultivated over the course of several few millennia. It would be naïve to evaluate China by only looking at the outer shell and considering the country's progress only according to Western standards.

The syncretism of Chinese culture alludes to a time when China had to adopt and adjust its modern science and diplomacy in order to deal with Westerners. Diplomacy was adjusted first; science was adjusted afterwards.

China adopted the functionality of European diplomacy to negotiate with Western powers during the period of imperialism of the 19th century. China had not yet established its own modern science, as Western forms of science were only brought to China a century after diplomacy was. In the 1990s, the Communist leadership declared that the Chinese people need to take an active part in the modern scientific and technological endeavours that belong to all of humankind.[273]

The syncretism of modern China has shown tremendous results. Within just the past few decades, China declared its serious intention to be a major international power, and its actions has shown it aims to expand its geopolitical acquisitions, pursue a leadership position in the world, and bring about a multipolar global system.

I suggest looking at this geopolitical change from the perspective of the traditional Chinese perceptions about science that constituted its national style. I then look at China's modern practices related to science diplomacy and evaluate China's endeavours in enhancing international scientific cooperation, fostering diplomatic interactions, and generating soft power. Finally, I evaluate China's potential in science diplomacy and its ambitions for global leadership.

8.2   *Chinese Syncretism*

The difference between Chinese science and science in the West is dramatic, and for the most part is due to the theoretical foundations upon which the scientific revolution occurred in Europe. In Europe, science was used to unveil the laws of nature or 'God's' laws. By contrast, the Chinese civilisation had much more metaphysical groundings. The Chinese way in science was driven by the harmony and syncretism of the *yin* and *yang* duality and the so-called *five phases* of metal, wood, water, fire, and earth. These ideas represented constantly shifting and repeating cycles, with no high conceptualisation of God as it existed in the European Christian traditions.[274]

There is also a symbolic communication and ambiguity of the Chinese language, as the Chinese were believed to "speak and write not in a scientific manner, but in confusion, by means of various claims and discourses".[275] Symbolic communication provides room for alternative interpretations, as the choice of translation is predetermined by the ideological context of the writer.[276]

---

273   Toby E. Huff, *The Rise of Early Modern Science* (Cambridge University Press, 2003), pp. 250, 252.

274   Ibid., p. 241.

275   Mary Laven, Mission to China. "Matteo Ricci and the Jesuit Encounter with the East" (The UK: Faber & Faber 2011), p. 239.

276   Toby E. Huff, *The Rise of Early Modern Science*, p. 294.

China's mode of thought and the conceptual organisation of time and space are looked at through the cycles of repetition,[277] rather than in the linear conception of the West. From the Western perspective, China's cyclic way of thinking and haziness of spoken and written language constitute national peculiarities, and only add ambiguity to China's system of educational attainment – a system that was exclusive to China until the end of the 19th century.[278]

China's mode of thinking and communication deterred the development of a persuasive power of diplomacy with Western powers, often making diplomatic negotiations unclear. Eventually, this ambiguity worked against China when the Western powers broke up its empire during the age of imperialism.

From the Western view, the failure of traditional Chinese civilisation to launch its own scientific revolution is also explained by the lack of intellectual autonomy of non-state actors – in other words the inability of universities, cities and towns to exist as autonomous entities. A popular social revolt against the influence of authority did not happen in China, possibly due to the absence of any academic institution able to resolve a divergence of political viewpoints.[279] China maintained a powerful state bureaucracy and rigid social structure, based on the hierarchical principles of a censorial system and extended authority over large territorial units.

The first modern universities emerged in China only in the early 20th century as a type of Western model adaptation, showcasing the essence of Chinese syncretism. For the first time in Chinese history, a variety of professionals in law, medicine, business, and science asserted themselves to be semi-independent from the state. However, the following proletarian cultural revolution under Mao Zedong brought down these professionals. Later, under Deng Xiaoping's leadership, science was strictly committed to Marxist-Leninist guidance,[280] which almost completely excluded the free inquiry foundation needed for scientific creativity and innovation. The 1990s were a turning point for China, with the country beginning a broad adaptation of modern science and technology. However, China still struggles to balance between academic freedom and state control.

China's traditional way of thinking and civilisational peculiarities lie behind much of its modern political organisation and patterns of behaviour. China adapted its own version of modern science and diplomacy only relatively recently, but such adaptation was necessary to smooth the process in dealing

---

277 Ibid., p. 292.
278 Ibid., p. 299.
279 Ibid., p. 319.
280 Ibid., p. 379.

with Western powers and to step forward on the path of scientific and technological progress. Perhaps, when China achieves its goal of bridging the scientific and technological gap with developed countries, as it has already done in economics, it might abandon the Western model and embrace values more in harmony with traditional Chinese civilisation. For now, China is attempting to utilise a toolbox of diplomacy in order to gain international acceptance.

In sum, China's civilisational peculiarities demonstrate the dominance of the authoritarian state over horizontal connections. The absence of autonomy in China contrasts the liberal culture of the West. Municipalities with self-governance and independent jurisdiction never occurred in China. The absence of a system of academic autonomy and high bureaucratic control prevented the emergence of academic freedom.

8.3   *The Toolbox of Diplomacy*

China's modernisation and development embraces the idea of gaining the acceptance of the international community, primarily the US, Europe, and Japan. When it comes to science diplomacy, China's leverage can be outlined in at least two ways: (1) international engagement through signing scientific and technological bilateral agreements that express the joint will to deepen exchanges and joint actions, and (2) generating smart power.

(1)   Initially, China engaged with the international community by sending Chinese students to Western universities, competitively pursuing joint scientific work and publications among young academics, maintaining relations with the growing Chinese scientific diaspora abroad, and by developing national science and technology parks, such as the Tsinghua University Science Park.[281] China's signing of international agreements was testimony to its openness to cooperation and marked China's entrance onto the world stage. In 2010, there were 30 protocols signed between China and the United States,[282] and number of United Nations conventions which China had ratified.

(2)   There is no visible indication that China prioritises science diplomacy as a toolbox to implement its foreign policy. Instead, there is clear recognition that the use of hard military power and economic resources for material rewards may not be a feasible basis for China to be recognised and genuinely accepted by the international (and scientific) community.

---

281   Elizabeth Economy, *The Third Revolution. Xi Jinping and the New Chinese State* (NY, New York: Oxford University Press, 2018), p. 143.

282   Pierre-Bruno Ruffini, *Science and Diplomacy: A New Dimension of International Relations*, p. 37.

Chinese authorities see the power of attraction, persusasion and cooperation as more rewarding in the long run, and therefore better prioritised in foreign policy.[283] The integrated approach of smart power is central to the foreign policy of China.[284]

China's ability to generate the soft power of attraction through cultural projection was started in earnest under the leadership of Hu Jintao, who was concerned with public diplomacy efforts.[285] China's main diplomatic endeavour in this space was the launching of Confucius Institutes that were represented by the network of cultural agencies and embassies overseas. By 2014, there were over 475 Confucius Institutes functioning in 126 countries.[286]

Although the idea of developing a cultural network abroad is similar to France's cultural centres, a problem arises for China from the style of governance and traditional regulations placed upon these cultural entities. Because of their affiliation with the Chinese government, the Confucius Institutes are mainly viewed with suspicion as propaganda agents of the Chinese Communist Party.[287] For example, in Sweden, the institutes were suspected of conducting political surveillance and secret propaganda activities. In Australia, some academics argued that the Confucius Institutes are a deliberate threat to liberal academic freedom.[288]

China's political system and traditional values are alien to Western liberalism, scientific autonomy and creativity. The Confucius Institutes will more likely be disregarded by liberal societies or, at the very least, viewed with greater suspicion. China instead targets Western values through foreign influence to gain the world's trust in socialism with Chinese characteristics.[289] Thus, China's capacity to generate soft power is limited by fundamental cultural differences when it comes to Western countries. The soft power of Chinese diplomacy has transformed into the 'sharp' power of economic influence, but this image will not attract cooperation due to the authoritarian political system and different values that lie behind it.[290]

---

283 Jeffrey Gil, 'China's Cultural Projection: A Discussion of the Confucius Institutes,' *China: An International Journal*, vol. 13, no. 1 (April 2015), p. 201.

284 Pierre-Bruno Ruffini, *Science and Diplomacy: A New Dimension of International Relations*, p. 14.

285 Elizabeth Economy, *The Third Revolution. Xi Jinping and the New Chinese State*, p. 7.

286 Falk Hartig, *Chinese Public Diplomacy* (London and New York: Routledge 2016), p. 2.

287 Ibid., p. 2.

288 Jeffrey Gil, 'China's Cultural Projection,' p. 220.

289 Elizabeth Economy, *The Third Revolution. Xi Jinping and the New Chinese State*, p. 39.

290 Falk Hartig, 'New Public Diplomacy Meets Old Public Diplomacy – the Case of China and Its Confucius Institutes," *New Global Studies*, vol. 8, issue 3 (2014), p. 331.

For some Western powers, China itself is a target of science diplomacy. For instance, China is a receiver of the UK Newton Fund. Some British universities have opened branches in China, such as the University of Nottingham in Ningbo. Switzerland has run the *swissnex* network in China as one of the established science diplomacy instruments of Swiss foreign policy. As Switzerland acknowledges, the obstacles that the *swissnex* networks in China face relate to a very different political, economic and cultural environment. China's complex administrative system, different way of doing business, and traditional values remain hurdles for the *swissnex* networks in China to succeed.[291] As a recipient of science diplomacy initiatives, China is perhaps pragmatic about the value of obtaining new experience.

The syncretism of China's civilisation characterises its national style in modern science. China might be led by its pragmatic syncretism and useful adaptation of advanced knowledge. Having different perceptions about espionage and the theft of intellectual property, might be an insurmountable barrier for genuine scientific collaboration between Chinese and Western researchers, and might also erode diplomatic negotiations as they are traditionally considered by the West.

While China's national endeavour in conducting smart power is notable, the country's state-centred approach to science dramatically limits its influence and the international community's receptiveness. If it chose to, China could utilise science diplomacy in the implementation of its foreign policy; however, there is currently no visible sign that this is occurring. Otherwise, China is pragmatically receptive to Western science diplomacy, even as it is conducted though a Western system of values.

Finally, Xi Jinping's ambitions for global leadership are based on the cohesive use of military power and China's economic prowess. Xi is pushing diplomacy towards multilateralism, and recognises that China must take on a greater share of the burden of global leadership alongside the US[292] and other Western powers. These ambitions might remain an obstacle for liberal Western powers seeking to build collaborative governance to address global problems on a systematic scale. Differences between China and the West exist in cultural values, perceptions about human rights, freedom of speech, ethics and morality, scientific autonomy and creativity, and intellectual property rights. While

---

291 Flavia Schlegel, Olivier Jacot & Marc Fetscherin, 'Science diplomacy with swissnex China: A Swiss nation brand initiative,' *Place Branding and Public Diplomacy*, vol. 7, issue 4 (November 2011), pp. 289-298.

292 Elizabeth Economy, *The Third Revolution. Xi Jinping and the New Chinese State*, p. 239.

NATIONAL STYLES IN SCIENCE, DIPLOMACY, AND SCIENCE DIPLOMACY 83

it is premature to say that China harbours any ambitions for global governance through science diplomacy, a reality that is unlikely to change in the near future, China's ambitions for global leadership can also not be neglected.

Conclusion: Science Diplomacy in Perspective

Diplomacy and science are in need of each other. When it comes to shaping the world order and addressing the global challenges of climate change, the risk of great power conflict, nuclear threats, global poverty and inequality – not to mention making interstate relations more effective and cooperative – what is needed is a diplomatic approach that can reduce the obstacles to shared understanding. Once differences between countries have been accepted, their activities will be accepted too. Countries' national styles in science and diplomacy indicate these differences. Fundamental traditions in both science and diplomacy still remain, making the identification of national traits possible, even as geopolitical change global problems make them evolve. The long legacy of tradition shapes countries' national styles in science and diplomacy, and reaches beyond both history and national borders. The concept of national style in science diplomacy has great analytical potential if effectively utilised by academics and practitioners.

When examining theory in IR and diplomacy through a Realist perspective, the concept of science diplomacy can be outlined through national interest, pragmatic statecraft, gaining influence, and maintaining the balance of power. A focus on science diplomacy takes this analysis even further, towards the long-term strategies of great powers in world politics. The P5 Countries, as great powers, might aim to maintain their positions of influence in international politics, gain more power, and then use collaborative governance to address global problems such as climate change and international inequality on a systematic scale.

Building good interstate relations and maintaining international influence is essential in making and reshaping world politics. Global leadership is based on the ability to achieve mutual understanding and share the benefits from a world with rising prosperity. The capacity to generate soft power through science diplomacy contributes enormously to the advancement of national strength through educational, scientific, or economic cooperation.

The role of *science diplomacy for global governance* is critical. What is thought of as a global problem is often the sum of local problems perceived as part of a more universal crisis. Local crises are now so often seen as instances of larger structural problems in international politics.[293] Global governance does not necessarily provide an indication of great powers' global dominance and influence. However, a realistic approach to solving local problems is to move towards larger spatial scales for understanding contemporary challenges. Giving a leading role to science diplomacy is fundamentally a way to make a global governance a possibility. Science diplomacy reflects the political actions through which great powers influence world politics.

Science diplomacy also operates and benefits from the increasing involvement of various institutions, states and non-state actors. This does not mean lessening the importance of nation-states. Governments remain the most powerful actors in the global system, but many new players can compete effectively in the realm of soft power of science diplomacy – the power to attract, persuade, and cooperate.

The UK, France, the US, and Russia all share a common viewpoint on science and diplomacy, and the structural implementation of both. While their strategies for implementing science diplomacy vary, the general view remains the same. On the other hand, China's focus on scientific and technological development, together with its economic power, military capability, and assertive foreign policy, has became a source of concern for the other great powers. China's view of science diplomacy is vague, however, and its national style in science diplomacy is difficult to identify.

A country's national style in science and diplomacy consists in the continuous production and reproduction of relations, and the process of bringing science and diplomacy into being. By acknowledging the national components, the methods and tools of science diplomacy can be used to form a system of multipolarity. Science diplomacy itself should be given more political agency in international affairs, to the point of the centralising particular scientific networks beyond states and regions.

Reflecting the above, it is worth evaluating the series of recognised elements that constitute national style. Such elements are listed in the tables. I propose further discussion on national styles with both academics and practitioners.

Table 1 demonstrates the main characteristics that can be distinguished as national characteristics in science, diplomacy, and science diplomacy of each discussed country. This series of elements should not be taken as unchangeable. However, the featured elements that are derived from countries' historical backgrounds, and which are shaped by community standards, do influence international behaviour. Characteristics of national styles help us understand a state's aspirations towards science diplomacy, and allow us to evaluate a

---

293   Jo Guldi & David Armitage, *The History Manifesto*, p. 37.

NATIONAL STYLES IN SCIENCE, DIPLOMACY, AND SCIENCE DIPLOMACY

TABLE 1   Distinct and recognisable characteristics of national style in science, diplomacy, and science diplomacy

↓Countries Elements of national style in→	Science	Diplomacy	Science diplomacy
UK	– Academic autonomy; – Pragmatism and practicality in conducting research; – Religiosity, ethics and morality in obtaining and implementing knowledge; – Dominance in the natural sciences; – Scientism and the spirit of education.	– 'Old diplomacy' of *Realism*; – Professional, selectively formed diplomatic corps; – Foreign policy implementation; – Forging geopolitical assemblages; – Brexit as diplomacy of possibility; – Aesthetic component of representation.	– Trendsetter and global leader; – Wide network of embassies and consulates that work jointly with non-state actors; – Investments in research and development with developed countries, (re)emerging scientific powers, and ODA recipients; – Effective soft power of scientific attractiveness; – Long-term strategy to build trust, gain commitments, and share collective responsibility; – High potential for global governance.
France	– Inseparability of science and state; – Traditions of public debate and scientific expertise; – Science as a career;	– Consular diplomacy as a tool to implement foreign policy; – 'Movement' diplomacy;	– Intersection between scientific diplomacy and cultural diplomacy; – Highly effective soft power of culture, science and education;

TABLE 1   Distinct and recognisable characteristics of national style in science (*cont.*)

↓Countries Elements of national style in→	Science	Diplomacy	Science diplomacy
France (*cont.*)	– Scientific hierarchy; – Traditional separation between 'generalists' and 'specialists'; – State control over research funding; – Historical continuity of *French science policy*.	– Diplomacy of 'cohabitation' or territorial diplomacy; – Limited public influence.	– Strong regional position in Europe; – Strong influence in the Global South; – Moderate ability for global governance.
US	– Academic autonomy; – Efficient industrial research and innovation; – The impact of the consumer culture on technological development; – Rational balancing between the public and personal good; – Rational balancing between academic freedom and public approval.	– Professional, intellectual and personified; – Politically forced ambassadorial diplomacy; – Theoretically and practically integrated; – Hawkish, farsighted and forward-deployed; – Emphasis on militarisation and economic power; – Emphasis on public diplomacy and public opinion; – Propagating liberal democracy and American values for global prosperity; – Tendentious focus on national exceptionalism and superiority.	– Trendsetter and global leader; – Receptive to public initiatives and the involvement of non-state actors; – Highly effective soft power of science and education; – High potential for global governance.

NATIONAL STYLES IN SCIENCE, DIPLOMACY, AND SCIENCE DIPLOMACY   87

TABLE 1   Distinct and recognisable characteristics of national style in science (*cont.*)

↓Countries Elements of national style in→	Science	Diplomacy	Science diplomacy
Russia	– The phenomenon of the 'Russian century;' – The phenomenon of *intelligentsia*; – State support, state control, and mostly centralised state funding; – Industry and defence seen as priorities; – Strong positions in mathematics, theoretical physics, and space sciences.	– Selectively formed diplomatic corps; – Pragmatic, realist, non-ideological, secret diplomacy; – Reflects the style of political leadership; – Network diplomacy; – 'Smart' but often antagonistic towards other powers; – Keen on public diplomacy to reinforce popular support but restrictive of public involvement.	– Historically a provider and initiator, but currently a receiver; – Lacks scientific attractiveness; – Strong potential to sustain good bilateral and multilateral relations embracing science diplomacy; – Moderate ability for global governance.
China	– Syncretism in adaptation of Western science and technology; – No academic autonomy.	– Syncretism in adaptation of Western diplomacy; – Strong top-down approach to foreign policy-making and implementation; – Hawkish, pragmatic.	– Smart and 'sharp' power of public diplomacy; – International scientific engagement; – Conditionally receptive to science diplomacy; – Aspirations for global leadership.

country's potential to use science diplomacy in the dimensions of bilateral relations, multilateral relations, and for global governance.

Table 2 evaluates the countries' capacity to use science diplomacy in the three dimensions:

- Maintaining bilateral relations, by which is meant the conduct of relations between two states with science diplomacy aspirations;
- Maintaining multilateral relations between three or more states as a mechanism by great powers to demonstrate their scientific attractiveness and ability to expand scientific cooperation;
- A state's tendency towards global governance, based on its scientific capability, geopolitical influence, and place in the system of international relations.

TABLE 2 A country's projected ability to secure and promote its foreign policy objectives using science diplomacy in the dimensions of bilateral relations, multilateral cooperation, and global governance (strong/moderate/weak)

↓Countries Science diplomacy use in→	bilateral relations	multilateral cooperation	global governance
UK	strong	strong	strong
France	strong	strong	moderate
US	strong	strong	strong
Russia	moderate	moderate	moderate
China	weak	weak	weak

My suggested results are based on the *hypotheses of state behaviour*. As expected, the UK and the US will likely keep leading positions in science diplomacy at all levels and develop each dimension further. France and Russia aim to keep their positions as regional stakeholders, and the aspirations of each towards global governance likely to remain rather moderate. China is a newcomer as an international player, yet demonstrates its ambitions for regional and global leadership. China's efforts for global governance will likely be confronted by the other great powers due to contrasting values and political aspirations.

•••

To conclude this study, I offer an argument in the classic *Realist* tradition formulated by John Mearsheimer. He argues that there should be a handful of great powers to balance a multipolar system in which no country has dominant military capacity.[294] This statement reflects not only the ideas of Realism as a theoretical framework, but also the current situation of ongoing geopolitical tensions, from Russia's ambition to secure its position as a meaningful regional player to China's determination to achieve regional and global dominance. Russia is unlikely to compete with either China or the US for global leadership, as the risk that Russia would lose would be too high. The UK aims to leverage its position for the benefit of global governance, while France seeks to strengthen its position on the European continent. These European powers maintain interstate relations with (re)emerging scientific powers and engage with the Global South.

More than any other country, it is the US who competes with China. Trade wars, economic pressure, and sabre-rattling are the most visible demonstrations of this competition. Any escalation of this competition might be dangerous and could lead to a reincarnation of the Cold War or even another round of great powers wars. Whatever it is that sparks natural and human-caused catastrophes this century will be of a totally different form to that which existed a few decades ago in the context of the Cold War. In this new global environment, any increase in geopolitical tensions puts at risk the entire human species. The potential to unite policy-makers and scientists within the framework of science diplomacy, and thereby choose a wise path forward for humanity, must be better understood, accepted, and skilfully embraced.

Effective science diplomacy has the real potential to decrease tensions between nations, find ways to improve people's lives, and, most fundamentally, bring the world closer to resolving those problems that humanity is capable of solving. While some scientific advances create new problems, others help find solutions. Diplomats have an important role to play in making the latter more common than the former, yet without scientific knowledge this would be hard to achieve. From gaining power and influence to strengthening bilateral and multilateral relations based on shared understanding, the potential of science diplomacy and national styles should not be overlooked.

• • •

Key findings:
– Continuous advancement in science is the foundation of a country's potential to apply science diplomacy tools in its foreign policy.

---

294   John J. Mearsheimer, *The Tragedy of Great Power Politics* (New York: Norton, 2001), p. 45.

- The inclusion of science diplomacy into a state's foreign policy agenda is an indicator of a state's leverage towards global governance, suggesting ways for the state to help resolve global problems, take responsibility for lesser powers, and showcase its growing global influence.
- Understanding and utilising science diplomacy objectives is a great aid in maintaining a peaceful balance of power, leaving a state's military capacity secondary to sophisticated policy and politics led by science.
- The hypotheses of state behaviour explain how great powers view science diplomacy objectives:
  - The US and the UK are the main initiators and contributors of science diplomacy in all its dimensions;
  - France extends its leverage in the mixture of scientific and cultural diplomacy mainly directed towards the Global South;
  - Russia lacks the ability to generate science diplomacy and does not prioritise initiatives for global governance, yet focuses on its role a regional stakeholder;
  - China's economic and military power is greatly expanding, yet Chinese science diplomacy is mostly invisible in a foreign policy agenda that prioritises the promotion of cultural heritage instead, for instance via the Confucius Institutions. China's leverage towards regional and global leadership is increasing, yet is likely be confronted by liberal democracies in the future.

Acknowledgement

The author wishes to thank Jeffrey Robertson for his advice on the earliest stage of this study.

References

Adamson, Matthew. 'Les liaisons dangereuses: resource surveillance, uranium diplomacy and secret French–American collaboration in 1950s Morocco,' *BJHS*, vol. 49, no. 1 (March 2016), pp. 79-105.

Armitage, David. 'The Atlantic Ocean' in David Armitage, Alison Bashford & Sujit Sivasundaram (ed.), *Oceanic Histories* (Cambridge University Press, 2018), pp. 85-110.

Aron, Raymond. *Peace and War: A Theory of International Relations* (New Brunswick, New Jersey: Transaction Publishers, 2003).

Balme, Richard. 'Revisiting French diplomacy in the age of globalization,' *French Politics*, vol. 8, no. 1, (2010), pp. 91-95.

Balter, Michael. 'Storming the Bastille,' *Science*, vol. 296 (26 April 2002), pp. 649-651.

Berridge, G. R. *Diplomacy. Theory and Practice* (The UK: Palgrave Macmillan, 2010).

Berridge, G. R. 'Machiavelli' in G. R. Berridge, Maurice Keens-Soper & T. G. Otte (ed.), *Diplomatic Theory from Machiavelli to Kissinger* (Palgrave, 2001).

Berridge, G. R., Maurice Keens-Soper & T. G. Otte (ed.), *Diplomatic Theory from Machiavelli to Kissinger* (Basingstoke: Palgrave, 2001).

Biberman, Yelena. 'The Politics of Diplomatic Service Reforms in Post-Soviet Russia,' *Political Science Quarterly*, vol. 126, no. 4, (2011), pp. 669-680.

Bjola, Corneliu & Markus Kornprobst, *Understanding International Diplomacy. Theory, practice and ethics* (New York, NY: Routledge, 2013).

Blanga, Yehuda U. "Between Two and Four': The French Initiative and the Multi-Power Diplomatic Initiatives to Resolve the Middle East Crisis,' *Diplomacy & Statecraft*, vol. 27, no. 1 (2016), pp. 93-120.

Butterfield, Herbert. 'The Balance of Power' in Herbert Butterfield and Martin Wigh (ed.), *Diplomatic Investigations. Essays in the Theory of International Politics* (Cambridge, Massachusetts: Harvard University Press, 1966).

Byford, Andy. 'Turning Pedagogy into a Science: Teachers and Psychologists in Late Imperial Russia (1897-1917),' in Michael Gordin, Karl Hall and Alexei Kojevnikov (ed.), *Intelligentsia Science: The Russian Century, 1860-1960, Osiris*, Second Series, vol. 23 (Chicago: The University of Chicago Press, 2008), pp. 50-81.

Ceccarelli, Leah. *On the Frontier of Science: An American Rhetoric of Exploration and Exploitation* (East Lansing, Michigan: Michigan State University, 2013).

Chalecki, Elizabeth L. 'Knowledge in Sheep's Clothing: How Science Informs American Diplomacy,' *Diplomacy & Statecraft*, vol. 19 (2008), pp. 1-19.

Chan, Gerald. *Chinese Perspectives on International Relations. A Framework for Analysis* (Palgrave Macmillan, 1999), pp. 140-143.

Clary, David C. 'A Scientist in the Foreign Office,' *Science & Diplomacy* (September 2013).

Cohen, Eliot A. *The big Stick. The Limits of Soft Power & the Necessity of Military Force* (New York, NY: Basic Books, 2016).

Colglazier, William. 'Science and Diplomacy,' *Science*, vol. 335 (17 February 2012), p. 775.

Constantinou, Costas M. & James Der Derian, 'Sustaining Global Hope: Sovereignty, Power and the Transformation of Diplomacy,' in Costas M. Constantinou and James Der Derian (ed.), *Sustainable Diplomacies* (The UK: Palgrave Macmillan 2010), pp. 1-22.

Copeland, Daryl. 'Science Diplomacy: What's It All About?' *CEPI-CIPS Policy* Brief 13 (November 2011).

Dar, Humaira. 'Nuclear Diplomacy: A Case Study of French and Pakistani Behaviour,' *Pakistan Vision*, vol. 18, no. 2 (2017), pp. 211-236.

Dasque, Isabelle. 'Diplomats and Diplomacy,' *Encyclopédie pour une histoire nouvelle de l'Europe*, (9 November, 2017).

Dasque, Isabelle. 'La diplomatie française au lendemain de la Grande Guerre. Bastion d'une aristocratie au service de l'État?' *Vingtième Siècle. Revue d'histoire*, 2008/3 (n° 99), pp. 33-49.

Devin, Guillaume. 'Burst Diplomacy The Diplomacies of Foreign Policy: Actors and Methods,' *Brazilian Political Science Review*, vol. 4, no. 2 (2010) pp. 60-77.

Dittmer, Jason. *Diplomatic Material: Affect, Assemblage, and Foreign Policy* (Duke University Press, 2017).

Dittmer, Jason & Fiona McConnell (ed.), *Diplomatic Cultures and International Politics: Translations, Spaces and Alternatives* (New York, NY: Routledge, 2017).

Dobbins, James. *Foreign Service: Five Decades on the Frontlines of American Diplomacy*, (Washington D.C.: Brookings Institution Press, 2017).

Economy, Elizabeth. *The Third Revolution. Xi Jinping and the New Chinese State* (NY, New York: Oxford University Press, 2018).

Ezell, Edward Clinton & Linda Neuman Ezell, *The Partnership, a History of the Apollo-Soyuz Test Project* (The US: NASA, 1978).

Fähnrich, Birte. 'Science diplomacy: Investigating the perspective of scholars on politics – science collaboration in international affairs,' *Public Understanding of Science* (2015), pp. 1-16.

Farrow, Ronan. *War on Peace: The End of Diplomacy and the Decline of American Influence*, (New York, London: W.W. Norton, 2018).

Fedoroff, Nina V. 'Science Diplomacy in the 21st Century,' *Cell*, 136 (9 January 2009), pp. 9-11.

Fink, Gerald R., Alan I. Leshner, & Vaughan C. Turekian, 'Science diplomacy with Cuba,' *Science*, vol. 344, issue 6188 (06 June 2014).

Flink, Tim & Ulrich Schreiterer, 'Science diplomacy at the intersection of S&T policies and foreign affairs: toward a typology of national approaches,' *Science and Public Policy*, vol. 37(9) (November 2010), pp. 665-677.

Gascoigne, John. 'Science and the British Empire from its Beginnings to 1850' in Brett M. Bennett & Joseph M. Hodge (ed.), *Science and Empire. Knowledge and Networks of Science across the British Empire, 1800-1970* (The UK: Palgrave Macmillan 2011).

Geeraerts, Gustaaf & Men Jing, 'International Relations Theory in China,' *Global Society*, vol. 15, no. 3 (2001), pp. 251-276.

Gil, Jeffrey. 'China's Cultural Projection: A Discussion of the Confucius Institutes,' *China: An International Journal*, vol. 13, no. 1 (April 2015), pp. 200-226.

Gordin, Michael, Karl Hall & Alexei Kojevnikov (ed.), *Intelligentsia Science: The Russian Century, 1860-1960, Osiris*, Second Series, vol. 23 (Chicago: The University of Chicago Press, 2008).

Gordin, Michael D. and Karl Hall, 'Introduction: Intelligentsia Science inside and outside Russia,' in Michael Gordin, Karl Hall and Alexei Kojevnikov (ed.), *Intelligentsia Science: The Russian Century, 1860-1960, Osiris*, Second Series, vol. 23 (Chicago: The University of Chicago Press, 2008), pp. 1-19.

Gordin, Michael. 'The Heidelberg Circle: German Inflections on the Professionalization of Russian Chemistry in the 1860s,' in Michael Gordin, Karl Hall & Alexei Kojevnikov (ed.), *Intelligentsia Science: The Russian Century, 1860-1960, Osiris*, Second Series, vol. 23 (Chicago: The University of Chicago Press 2008), pp. 23-46.

Graham, Loren R. 'Big Science in the Last Years of the Big Soviet Union,' *Osiris*, 7 (1992), pp. 49-71.

Graham, Loren R. *Science in Russia and the Soviet Union. A Short History* (Cambridge University Press, 1993).

Graham, Loren R. 'When Ideology and Controversy Collide: The Case of Soviet Science,' *The Hastings Center Report*, vol. 12, no. 2 (April 1982), pp. 26-32.

Grieco, Joseph M. 'The Maastricht Treaty, Economic and Monetary Union and the Neo-Realist Research Programme,' *Review of International Studies*, vol. 21, no. 1 (January 1995), pp. 21-40.

Grimes, Robin W. & Claire McNulty, 'The Newton Fund: Science and Innovation for Development and Diplomacy,' *Science & Diplomacy* (December 2016).

Guldi, Jo & David Armitage, *The History Manifesto* (The UK: Cambridge University Press, 2014).

Gunitsky, Seva. 'Complexity and Theories of Change in International Politics,' *International Theory*, vol. 5, no. 1 (2013), pp. 35-63.

Haass, Richard. *A World in Disarray: American Foreign Policy and the Crisis of the Old Order: American Foreign Policy and the Crisis of the Old Order* (Penguin Books, 2018).

Hanson, Thomas. 'The Traditions and Travails of Career Diplomacy in the United States,' in Paul Sharp and Geoffrey Wiseman (ed.), *American Diplomacy* (Koninklijke Brill NV, Leiden, The Netherlands 2012), pp. 199-216.

Harrison, Carol & Ann Johnson (ed.), *National Identity: The Role of Science and Technology, Osiris*, vol. 24 (2009).

Harrison, Carol & Ann Johnson, 'Introduction: science and national identity,' in *Science and National Identity*, Osiris vol. 24, no. 1 (The University of Chicago Press, 2009), pp. 1-14.

Hartig, Falk. *Chinese Public Diplomacy* (London and New York: Routledge 2016).

Hartig, Falk. 'New Public Diplomacy Meets Old Public Diplomacy – the Case of China and Its Confucius Institutes," *New Global Studies*, vol. 8, issue 3 (2014), pp. 331-352.

Harwood, Jonathan. 'National Styles in Science: Genetics in Germany and the United States between the World Wars,' *Isis*, vol. 78 (1987), pp. 390-414.

Hassner, Pierre. 'Frustrated but Frozen: Europe and the Atlantic Relationship,' *International Journal*, vol. 39, no. 2 (1984), pp. 410-428.

Hassner, Pierre. 'Raymond Aron: Too Realistic to Be a Realist?' *Constellations*, vol. 14, no. 4 (2007), pp. 498-505.

Hassner, Pierre. 'Russia's Transition to Autocracy,' *Journal of Democracy*, vol. 19, no. 2 (April 2008), pp. 5-15.

Held, David, Anthony McGrew, David Goldblatt & Jonathan Perraton, *Global Transformations: Politics, Economics, and Culture* (Stanford University Press, 1999).

Hoffman, Philip T. 'Why Was It Europeans Who Conquered the World?' *The Journal of Economic History*, vol. 72, no. 3 (September 2012), pp. 601-633.

Hoffmann, Stanley. 'Raymond Aron and the Theory of International Relations,' *International Studies Quarterly*, vol. 29, no. 1 (March 1985), pp. 13-27.

Hogg, Jonathan & Christoph Laucht, 'Introduction: British nuclear culture,' *BJHS*, vol. 45, no. 4 (December 2012), pp. 479-493.

Holmes, Alison & J. Simon Rofe, *Global Diplomacy: Theories, Types, and Models* (Boulder, CO: Westview Press, 2016).

Holmes, Marcus, *Face-to-Face Diplomacy. Social Neuroscience and International Relations* (The UK: Cambridge University Press, 2018).

Hotez, Peter J. 'Russian–United States Vaccine Science Diplomacy: Preserving the Legacy', *PLoS Negl Trop Dis*, 11(5): e0005320.

Hotez, Peter J. '"Vaccine Diplomacy": Historical Perspectives and Future Directions', *PLoS Negl Trop Dis*, 8(6): e2808.

Huff, Toby E. *The Rise of Early Modern Science* (Cambridge University Press, 2003).

Ibragimova, K. A., 'EU Science Diplomacy and Framework Programmes as Instruments of STI Cooperation,' *MGIMO Review on International Relations*, vol. 5(56) (2017), pp. 151-168. (In Russian).

Ibragimova, K. A. & O. N. Barabanov, 'About the Prospects of the Russian Science Diplomacy,' *Vestnik RFFI* [Russian Foundation for Basic Research Herald], no 1 (97) (January-March 2018), pp. 57-59.

Ismailov, A. I. & K. K. Bazarbayev, 'History and Traditions of Russian Diplomacy,' *Historical Sciences*, no. 6 (2012), p. 5, (in Russian).

Jervis, Robert. 'Realism, Neoliberalism, and Cooperation: Understanding the Debate' in Colin Elman & Miriam Fendius Elman (ed.), *Progress in International Relations Theory. Appraising the Field* (The US: MIT Press 2003).

Jönsson, Christer. 'Global Governance: Challenges to Diplomatic Communication, Representation, and Recognition' in Andrew F. Cooper, Brian Hocking & William Maley (ed.), *Global Governance and Diplomacy. Worlds Apart?* (The UK: Palgrave Macmillan, 2008).

Just, Tony. *The Burden of Responsibility. Blum, Camus, Aron, and the French Twentieth Century* (Chicago and London: The University of Chicago Press, 1998).

Kagan, Korina. 'The Myth of the European Concert: The Realist-Institutionalist Debate and Great Power Behavior in the Eastern Question, 1821-41,' *Security Studies*, vol. 7, no. 2 (1997), pp. 1-57.

Kahler, Miles. 'Global Governance: Three Futures,' *International Studies Review*, vol. 20 (2018), pp. 239-246.

Keiger, John. 'Wielding Finance as a Weapon of Diplomacy: France and Britain in the 1920s,' *Contemporary British History*, vol. 25, no. 1, (2011), pp. 29-47.

Kennan, George F. *American Diplomacy: Sixtieth-Anniversary Expanded Edition* (The University of Chicago Press, 2012).

Kissinger, Henry. *Diplomacy* (New York, NY: Simon & Schuster, 1994).

Kissinger, Henry. *World* Order (Penguin Books, 2015).

Knight, David. *The Age of Science* (Oxford: Basil Blackwell, 1986).

Krasnyak, Olga. 'Science Diplomacy: An Underestimated Toolkit of South Korea's Foreign Policy,' *On Korea: Academic Paper Series 2018, Korea Economic Institute of America* (12 April 2018), p. 4.

Krasnyak, Olga. 'The Apollo-Soyuz Test Project: Construction of an Ideal Type of Science Diplomacy,' *The Hague Journal of Diplomacy*, vol. 13, no. 4 (2018).

Kuznetsov, Alexandr. "Inheriting legends sanctified by the time ...' From the history of the Russian foreign policy doctrine,' *Politia*, no. 4 (2004), p. 2, (in Russian).

Lane, Philippe. *French Scientific and Cultural Diplomacy*, (The UK: Liverpool University Press, 2013).

Laven, Mary. *Mission to China. Matteo Ricci and the Jesuit Encounter with the East* (The UK: Faber & Faber 2011).

Lavrov, Sergey. 'Russia's Foreign Policy in a Historical Perspective,' *Russia in Global Affairs* (20 March 2018).

Lebedeva, Marina M. & Maxim V. Kharkevich, 'Theory of International Relations in the Mirror of Contemporary Russian International Studies,' *MGIMO Review on International Relations*, vol. 5(50) (2016), pp. 7-19, (in Russian).

Lloyd, Davis & Robert G. Patman (ed.), *Science Diplomacy: New Day or False Dawn?* (World Scientific Publishing Company, 2015).

Lord, Kristin M. & Vaughan C. Turekian, 'Time for a New Era of Science Diplomacy,' *Science, New Series*, vol. 315, no. 5813 (9 February, 2007), pp. 769-770.

Lundborg, Tom. 'The ethics of neorealism: Waltz and the time of international life,' *European Journal of International Relations* (2018).

Manela, Erez. 'A Pox on Your Narrative: Writing Disease Control into Cold War History,' *Diplomatic History*, vol. 34, no. 2 (April 2010), pp. 299-323.

Mayer, Anna-K. 'Setting up a discipline, II: British history of science and "the end of ideology," 1931-1948,' *Studies in History and Philosophy of Science*, vol. 35 (2004), pp. 41-72.

McKercher, B. J. C. 'The Foreign Office, 1930-39: Strategy, Permanent Interests and National Security,' *Contemporary British History*, vol. 18, no. 3 (2004), pp. 87-109.

McKinney, Larry. 'Continue U.S.–Cuban science diplomacy,' *Science*, vol. 358, issue 6370 (22 Dec 2017), p. 1549.

Mearsheimer, John J. 'Introduction' in George F. Kennan, *American Diplomacy: Sixtieth-Anniversary Expanded Edition* (The University of Chicago Press 2012).

Mearsheimer, John J. *The Tragedy of Great Power Politics* (New York: W. W. Norton, 2014).

Mearsheimer, John J. *Great Delusion: Liberal Dreams and International Realities* (Yale University Press, 2018).

Milne, David. *Worldmaking: The Art and Science of American Diplomacy* (NY: Farrar, Straus and Giroux, 2017).

Milner, Anthony. 'Culture and the international relations of Asia,' *The Pacific Review*, vol. 30, no. 6 (2017), pp. 857-869.

Moedas, Carlos. 'Science Diplomacy in the European Union,' *Science & Diplomacy* (March 2016).

Moreno, Ana Elorza et. al. 'Spanish Science Diplomacy: A Global and Collaborative Bottom-Up Approach,' *Science & Diplomacy* (March 2017).

Morgenthau, Hans J. *Scientific Man vs. Power Politics* (Great Britain: Latimer House Limited, 1947).

Murray, Stuart et. al. 'The Present and Future of Diplomacy and Diplomatic Studies,' *International Studies Review*, vol. 13 (2011), pp. 709-728.

Nicolson, Harold. *Diplomacy* (Oxford University Press, 1942).

Niebuhr, Reinhold. *Moral Man and Immoral Society: A Study in Ethics and Politics* (New York City, NY: Charles Scribner's Sons, 1932).

Nye, Joseph. *Soft Power – The Means to Success in World Politics* (New York: PublicAffairs, 2009).

Nye, Joseph. 'How Sharp Power Threatens Soft Power,' *Foreign Affairs* (24 January, 2018).

Nye, Mary Jo. 'National Styles? French and English Chemistry in the Nineteen and Early Twentieth Centuries,' *Osiris* 2, no. 8 (1993), pp. 30-49.

Nye, Mary Jo. 'Recent Sources and Problems in the History of French Science,' *Historical Studies in the Physical Sciences*, vol. 13, no. 2 (1983), pp. 401-415.

Nye, Mary Jo. 'The Republic vs. The Collective: Two Histories of Collaboration and Competition in Modern Science,' *N.T.M.*, vol. 24 (2016), pp. 169-194.

Nye, Mary Jo. 'What price politics? Scientists and political controversy,' *Endeavour*, vol. 23, no. 4 (1999), pp. 148-154.

Opondo, Sam Okoth. 'Decolonizing Diplomacy: Reflections on African Estrangement and Exclusion,' in Costas M. Constantinou & James Der Derian (ed.), *Sustainable Diplomacies* (The UK: Palgrave Macmillan 2010), pp. 109-127.

Otte, T. G. 'Nicolson' in G. R. Berridge, Maurice Keens-Soper & T. G. Otte (ed.), *Diplomatic Theory from Machiavelli to Kissinger* (Basingstoke: Palgrave, 2001).

Otte, T. G. 'Old Diplomacy: Reflections on the Foreign Office before 1914,' *Contemporary British History*, vol. 18, no. 3, (2004), pp. 31-52.

Pamment, James. 'The Mediatization of Diplomacy,' *The Hague Journal of Diplomacy*, vol. 9 (2014), pp. 253-280.

Pickett, Warren E., Anthony J. Leggett & Paul C. W. Chu, 'Science Diplomacy with Iran,' *Nature Physics*, vol. 10 (July 2014), pp. 465-467.

Polyakova, Alina & Benjamin Haddad, 'Europe in the New Era of Great Power Competition. How the EU Can Stand Up to Trump and China,' *Foreign Affairs* (17 July, 2018).

Pouliot, Vincent. *International Security in Practice: The Politics of NATO-Russia Diplomacy* (UK, Cambridge: Cambridge University Press, 2010).

Proud, Virginia. 'The Hunt for Science Diplomacy: Practice and Perceptions in the Horizon 2020 Scientific community,' *EL-CSID Working Paper*, issue 2018/18 (June 2018).

Pyenson, Lewis. 'An end to national science: the meaning and the extension of local knowledge,' *History of Science*, vol. 40 (2002), pp. 251-290.

Qin, Yaqing. 'Development of International Relations Theory in China: Progress Through Debates,' *International Relations of the Asia-Pacific*, vol. 11 (2011), pp. 231-257.

Rathbun, Brian C. *Diplomacy's Value: Creating Security in 1920s Europe and the Contemporary Middle East* (Ithaca, NY: Cornell University Press, 2014).

Reingold, Nathan. 'National Styles in the Sciences: The United States Case,' in E. G. Forbes (ed.), *Human Implications of Scientific Advance* (Edinburgh: Edinburgh Univ. Press, 1978), pp. 163-173.

Reus-Smit, Christian. 'Cultural Diversity and International Order,' *International Organization*, vol. 71 (2017), pp. 851-885.

Robertson, Jeffrey. *Diplomatic Style and Foreign Policy: A Case Study of South Korea* (London and New York: Routledge, 2016).

Robertson, Jeffrey. 'Middle-power definitions: confusion reigns supreme,' *Australian Journal of International Affairs*, vol. 71, no. 3 (March 2017), pp. 1-16.

Roman, Alea Lopes De San & Simon Schutz, 'Understanding European Union Science Diplomacy,' *Journal of Common Market Studies* (2017), pp. 1-20.

Roman, Joe, James Kraska, 'Reboot Gitmo for U.S.-Cuba research diplomacy,' *Science*, vol. 351, issue 6279 (18 Mar 2016), pp. 1258-1260.

Romanova, M. D. 'Science Diplomacy: Dimensions and Practices,' *Science, Innovation, Education* [Nauka, Innovatsii, Obrazovanie], no. 1 (23) 2017, pp. 38-52, (in Russian).

Rostow, W. W. 'The American National Style,' *Daedalus*, vol. 87, no. 2 (Spring 1958), pp. 110-144.

Rüffin, Nicolas & Ulrich Schreiterer, 'Case Study Science and Technology Agreements in the Toolbox of Science Diplomacy: Effective Instruments or Insignificant Add-ons?' *EL-CSID Working Paper*, issue 2017/6 (September 2017).

Ruffini, Pierre-Bruno. *Science and Diplomacy: A New Dimension of International Relations* (Berlin: Springer, 2017).

Schmid, Sonja D. 'Organizational Culture and Professional Identities in the Soviet Nuclear Power Industry,' in Michael Gordin, Karl Hall and Alexei Kojevnikov (ed.), *Intelligentsia Science: The Russian Century, 1860-1960, Osiris*, Second Series, vol. 23 (Chicago: The University of Chicago Press 2008), pp. 82-111.

Schlegel, Flavia, Olivier Jacot & Marc Fetscherin, 'Science diplomacy with swissnex China: A Swiss nation brand initiative,' *Place Branding and Public Diplomacy*, vol. 7, issue 4 (November 2011), pp. 289-298.

Sending, Ole Jacob, Vincent Pouliot & Iver B. Neumann, 'The Future of Diplomacy,' *International Journal*, vol. 66, no. 3 (2011), pp. 527-542.

Shakleyina, Tatyana A. & Aleksei D. Bogaturov, 'Russian Realist School of International Relations,' *Communist and Post-Communist Studies*, vol. 37, issue 1 (March 2004), pp. 37-51.

Shestopal, Alexei V. & Nikolay V. Litvak, 'Science Diplomacy: French Experience,' *MGIMO Review on International Relations*, vol. 5(50) (2016), pp. 106-114. (In Russian).

Sharp, Paul. *Diplomatic Theory of International Relations* (Cambridge University Press, 2009).

Sharp, Paul & Geoffrey Wiseman (ed.), *American Diplomacy* (Koninklijke Brill NV, Leiden, The Netherlands, 2012).

Siddiqi, Asif A. 'Competing Technologies, National(ist) Narratives, and Universal Claims: Toward a Global History of Space Exploration,' *Technology and Culture*, vol. 51, no. 2 (April 2010), pp. 425-443.

Siddiqi, Asif A. 'Imagining the Cosmos: Utopians, Mystics, and the Popular Culture of Spaceflight in Revolutionary Russia,' in Michael Gordin, Karl Hall and Alexei Kojevnikov (ed.), *Intelligentsia Science: The Russian Century, 1860-1960. Osiris*, Second Series, vol. 23 (Chicago: The University of Chicago Press 2008), pp. 260-288.

Singer, Peter. *Ethics in the Real World: 82 Brief Essays on Things That Matter* (Princeton University Press, 2016).

Sivovolov, Dmitry. 'The Role of Russian Diplomacy in the Construction of 'Electronic Governmet' in Russia,' *MGIMO Review on International Relations*, [Vestrnik MGIMO] vol. 5 (32) (2013), pp. 54-57, (in Russian).

Spangenburg, Ray & Diane Kit Moser, *Modern Science, 1896-1945* (New York, NY: Facts On File, Inc. 2004).

Spence, David. 'Taking Stock: 50 Years of European Diplomacy,' *The Hague Journal of Diplomacy*, vol. 4 (2009), pp. 235-259.

Streltsov, Dmitry & Artem Lukin, 'Russian-Japanese Rapprochement Through the Lens of IR theory. Neo-classical Realism, Constructivism, and Two Level Games,' *International Trends*, vol. 15, no. 2 (April-June 2017), pp. 44-63, (in Russian).

Swire, Hugo. 'The UK, Brazil and Science Diplomacy,' a speech delivered on 15 December 2014.

Taylor, Brendan. *The Four Flashpoints: How Asia Goes to War* (Australia: La Trobe University Press, 2018).

Trager, Robert F. *Diplomacy: Communication and the Origins of International Order* (The UK: Cambridge University Press, 2017).

Trenn, Thaddeus. 'The central role of energy in Soddy's holistic and critical approach to nuclear science, economics, and social responsibility,' *BJHS*, vol. 12 (1979), pp. 261-276.

Tsygankov, Andrei. *The Russian International Theory: The Three Traditions* (Russia, Moscow: RuScience 2018), (in Russian).

Van Langenhove, Luk. 'Tools for an EU Science Diplomacy' (Luxembourg: Publications Office of the European Union, 2017).

Van Langenhove, Luk & Elke Boers, 'Science Diplomacy in search of a purpose in the populist era,' *United Nations University Institute on Comparative Regional Integration Studies (UNU-CRIS)*, issue 2018/4 (March 2018).

Van Langenhove, Luk. 'Global Science Diplomacy for Multilateralism 2.0,' *Science & Diplomacy*, vol. 5, no. 3 (December 2016).

Walker, Mark. 'The 'national' in international and transnational science,' *BJHS*, vol. 45, no. 3 (September 2012), pp. 359-376.

Walsh, John. 'Some New Targets Defined for French Science Policy,' *Science*, vol. 156 (5 May 1967), pp. 626-631.

Walzt, Kenneth. *Theory in International Politics* (Addison-Wesley, 1979).

Wang, Yiwei. 'China. Between copying and constructing' in Arlene B. Tickner & Ole Wæver (ed.), *International Relations. Scholarship Around the World* (New York, NY: Routledge, 2009), pp. 103-119.

Wendt, Alexander. *Social Theory of International Politics* (The UK: Cambridge University Press, 1999).

Wessely, Anna. 'Transposing 'Style' from the History of Art to the History of Science,' *Science in Context*, vol. 4 (1991), pp. 265-278.

Wiseman, Geoffrey. 'Distinctive Characteristics of American Diplomacy,' *The Hague Journal of Diplomacy*, vol. 6 (2011), pp. 235-259.

Wiseman, Geoffrey. 'Evolution of (my) thinking about diplomatic culture,' ISA Annual convention San Francisco 2018, conference paper.

Wiseman, Geoffrey. 'Pax Americana: Bumping into Diplomatic culture,' *International Studies Perspectives*, vol. 6, (2005), pp. 409-430.

Xuetong, Yan. 'Chinese Values vs. Liberalism: What Ideology Will Shape the International Normative Order?' *The Chinese Journal of International Politics*, (2018), pp. 1-22.

Yakushiji, Taizo. 'The Potential of Science and Technology Diplomacy,' *Asia-Pacific Review*, vol. 16 (1) (2009), pp. 1-7.

Young, J. W. 'Review article. French Diplomacy,' *History*, vol. 75, issue 245 (October 1990), pp. 425-429.

Ziegler, Charles E. 'Diplomacy' in Andrei P. Tsygankov (ed.), *Routledge Handbook of Russian Foreign Policy* (New York, NY: Routledge, 2018).

Zonova, Tatiana V. 'Diplomatic Cultures: Comparing Russia and the West in Terms of a 'Modern Model of Diplomacy," *The Hague Journal of Diplomacy*, vol. 2 (2007), pp. 1-23.

Reports

The AAAS & The Royal Society, 'New frontiers in science diplomacy' (2010).

Government of Spain, 'Report on Science, Technology, and Innovation Diplomacy' (2016).

Houses of Parliament, 'Science Diplomacy,' number 568 (February 2018).

National Academy of Sciences, 'U.S. and International Perspectives on Global Science Policy and Science Diplomacy: Report of a Workshop' (2012).

The White House, 'National Security Strategy of the United States of America' (December 2017).

Printed in the United States
By Bookmasters